THE PENSIONS R[...]

An Employer's Guide

THE PENSIONS REVOLUTION

An Employer's Guide

Norman Toulson

KOGAN PAGE

To Diana

© Norman Toulson 1988

All rights reserved. No reproduction, copy or transmission of this publication may be made without written permission.

No paragraph of this publication may be reproduced, copied or transmitted save with written permission or in accordance with the provisions of the Copyright Act 1956 (as amended), or under the terms of any licence permitting limited copying issued by the Copyright Licensing Agency, 7 Ridgmount Street, London WC1E 7AE.

Any person who does any unauthorised act in relation to this publication may be liable to criminal prosecution and civil claims for damages.

Fist published in 1988 by
Kogan Page Ltd,
120 Pentonville Road, London N1 9JN

British Library Cataloguing in Publication Data

Toulson, Norman, *1920*
  The pensions revolution : an employers guide.
  1. Great Britain. Companies. Superannuation schemes
  I. Title
  331.25'2'0941

ISBN 1 85091 763 9
ISBN 1 85091 764 7 Pbk

Photoset in North Wales by
Derek Doyle & Associates, Mold, Clwyd
Printed and bound in Great Britain by
Biddles Ltd, Guildford and King's Lynn

Contents

Preface 7
Introduction 9
   Everybody needs a pension 9
   Job mobility demands flexibility of pensions 10
   The pensions revolution offers flexibility 11
   All employers have a vital part to play 11
   The element of chance 12
   Unbiased advice 13

1. **What are the Choices?** 15
   SERPS 15
   Contracting out or living on top 17
   Employers' schemes 18
   Personal pensions 22

2. **How Flexible are the Choices?** 25
   SERPS 25
   Occupational pensions 27
   Personal pensions 28
   Other flexibilities 30

3. **Who Pays?** 31
   SERPS 32
   Employers' schemes 32
   Personal pensions 34

4. **What Tax Angles are There?** 37
   SERPS 37
   Inland Revenue approval of other pension sources 38
   Tax relief on employer's contributions 41
   Tax relief on employees' contributions 42
   Investment income and capital gains 42
   Taxation of benefits 43

5. **Should an Employer Try to Influence Employees' Choices?** 45
   Dangers of under- and over-involvement 45
   The attitudes of younger and older employees 46
   The attitudes of some married women employees 47
   The attitudes of part-time employees 48
   Putting everybody in the picture 48
   Inducements to belong to a scheme 50

6. **How Should Pension Funds be Invested?** 53
   Personal pensions 54
   Money purchase occupational schemes 63
   Self-administered occupational schemes 64
   Insured defined benefits schemes 67
   Comparing providers 68

7. **Should One Contract Out?** 71
   Possible routes to contracting out 71
   Larger contributions may reduce expenses 73
   The five-year initial boost 74
   Changing pension providers 75
   A note of caution 75

8. **What Choice Will You Make? (Checklists for employers)** 77
   Checks on occupational scheme provisions 78
   Checks on possible treatment of employees who leave an employer's scheme or refuse to join one 79
   Checks on effectiveness of communication with employees 80

Appendix 81
   Summary of the Principal Inland Revenue Limits on Benefits Under Occupational Pension Schemes – Except on Leaving Service

Glossary 89
Index 101

Preface

Freedom for employees to choose the source of their retirement benefits is now a fact of life. This may be a privilege, but it offers more scope for making the wrong choice than the right one. There are so many sources available.

No employer wants employees to choose unwisely. Unwise decisions today may lead to regrets and poor morale tomorrow. Caring employers will want to help their employees deal with high-pressure salesmen attempting to stampede them into buying personal pensions irrespective of whether they improve or worsen their pension prospects. Thanks to the Financial Services Act, the number of unscrupulous salesmen may be fairly small, but it would be unrealistic to think that there will be none. A few words of warning might help employees to see any flaws in a salesman's argument, whether he is reckless or over-enthusiastic.

Nobody can guarantee to point an employee infallibly in the right direction. I have tried to present a fair and adequate picture of the possibilities, while omitting various matters of detail which may distract attention from general principles. I have written a book which should help you, as an employer, to decide how you can help your employees to make responsible use of their freedom of choice. This applies whether you yourself have a pension scheme for them or not.

For the sake of simplicity, I have addressed the book primarily to employers with a modest number of employees. Occasional comments point out where the opportunities or difficulties of an employer with a large staff are different.

My practice of referring to an employee as 'he' or 'him' does not stem from male chauvinism. I think it is neater than the use of 'he or she' or referring to an individual as 'they' or 'them'. And it is acceptable to Bridget Boyle, who has kindly read the manuscript and made several valuable suggestions. They have greatly improved the book, and I am very grateful to her for them.

Norman Toulson
May 1988

Introduction

Many critics see changes brought about by the Social Security Act 1986 as the Government's attempt to privatise SERPS. While there is a measure of truth in this, there is an additional – and more important – objective, which the Government shares with its predecessors. Nearly half of the nation's earners rely on the state alone to provide them with an income in retirement. What the state provides is determined by a succession of Social Security Acts. The Government hopes that the 1986 Act will help to increase greatly the number of people whose total pensions exceed what reliance on earlier Acts would provide.

Everybody needs a pension

Eliza Doolittle may only have wanted 'a room somewhere, far away from the cold night air, with one enormous chair'. But somebody who is retired needs a pension too. So does a widow whose husband's death has deprived her of a share of his earnings or pension.

Few teenagers and people in their twenties take any interest in the prospect of drawing a pension in 30 or

40 years' time. As the years pass, the idea of retirement as a future way of life begins to take shape: almost imperceptibly it changes from being a possibility to being a probability. Some people sweep it under the carpet; some are so busy thinking about other things that they pay little attention to it. But like a slow-moving, distant railway train, retirement approaches with increasing rapidity until it arrives at breakneck speed.

In one's late fifties, when some contemporaries are taking early retirement either because they need a quieter life or because they have been invited to make way for younger men, the need for something to live on in retirement makes itself apparent as a fact of life. Pay days are numbered and will soon be a thing of the past. What will take their place? If a good pension is in the offing, one of the most insistent worries about retirement vanishes.

Job mobility demands flexibility of pensions

The world in which people joined an employer immediately after leaving school and stayed with him until advancing years called a halt is vanishing. The search for greater experience or promotion makes many ambitious people move from one employer to another – possibly several times. Takeovers, amalgamations and changes in consumer demand lead to redundancies and a search for new employment.

Whether these changes occur early or late in an employee's working life, they may seriously affect income in retirement unless his pension arrangements make adequate allowance for them. Since the early 1970s, Social Security legislation has progressively improved the lot of the job-changer, but some types of pension provision favour him more than others.

The pensions revolution offers flexibility

The Social Security Act 1973 introduced compulsory preservation of pension scheme benefits payable at or after retirement for all members of their employers' occupational pension schemes who left after completing five years' qualifying service and attaining the age of 26. The Social Security Pensions Act 1975 – the initial state earnings related pension legislation – ensured that such a pension, or its contracted-out equivalent, would be preserved and revalued to take account of inflation if a member changed jobs. Inflation still eroded the preserved pensions in excess of SERPS for many people.

The Social Security Act 1985 remedied that situation to some extent for members who leave after 1 January 1986. The greater the gap between that date and the date of leaving, the more effective the remedy will be.

The 1986 Act institutes another element of flexibility. It allows the earner to decide whether to join his employer's pension scheme (if there is one), whether to leave the scheme if he is already a member, and whether to arrange a personal pension if for any reason he is not in an employer's scheme.

All employers have a vital part to play

The Government is running a campaign to publicise this latest extension to flexibility. It includes two DHSS leaflets for employees, entitled 'New pensions choices'. NP41 contains a considerable amount of information: NP40 is the abridged version. Copies of both leaflets, and of NP42 for employers, are available from the Leaflets Unit, PO Box 21, Stanmore, Middlesex HA7 1AY.

It is safe to assume that the majority of employees will not see either leaflet unless somebody gives them a copy. And the majority of those who do receive a copy will not study it unless somebody gives them a strong incentive to do so. It is also regrettably certain that many employees will find themselves the targets of salesmen who explain convincingly why they should adopt whatever method of pension provision suits the salesmen's pockets. For all these reasons, an employer may find, sooner or later, that employee morale is suffering.

To reduce the risk of this happening, why not consider how you can help your employees to take an informed look at the choices which they could make? If you have a pension scheme you could take a detached view of what it offers so as to see whether you could usefully update it. You could also consider how most effectively to draw the attention of the members to the ways in which it improves upon the alternatives. If you have not installed a scheme, you could explore the new opportunities the 1986 Act offers you for benefiting your employees at modest cost. This book will give you some ideas about how to give your employees a better chance of making the right choice.

The element of chance

The eventual effect of choosing each of the alternatives an employee may have depends on several variable factors. Nobody can predict with certainty *how* the factors will vary and what effect changes will have in a particular case, but the following paragraphs mention possible areas of change which deserve thought.

Each of the factors may be affected to some extent by changes in the law. Any general election may lead to a change of government and a corresponding change in pensions policy.

The amounts of the eventual benefits which most of the choices will provide depend on how profitably contributions to the funds are invested. Comparing rates of interest which have been obtainable in recent years with the rate of 2.5 per cent per annum which applied for a short period in the late 1940s gives an indication of how enormous long-term fluctuations can be. Interest rates tend to be high when the rate of inflation is high, but it cannot be assumed that the investment income of a fund will enable it to increase benefits to as great an extent as a government can increase state benefits out of taxation. Nor can it be assumed that the investment income will depend solely on the economic climate. Government controls on how funds could be invested might alter their investment yield.

Even within a given environment, there will be considerable variations between the effectiveness of the investment programmes of different fund managers. Also, the cost of administration varies from one fund to another.

Given all these uncertainties, nobody can guarantee that any route to pension provision will be the most generally effective over a particular period. In addition, the unique circumstances of any individual reduces the scope for accurate prediction even further: an accident, an illness or the collapse of an employer's business may disrupt plans severely.

Unbiased advice

In view of the difficulty of knowing how best to choose, is there any point in an employee's making a choice? Staying where one is may be wiser than trying to improve one's prospects by making a change.

There are undoubtedly circumstances in which this is true, but there are also people for whom staying put is guaranteed to be the worst choice. As a future pensioner each employee would be well advised to make sure that he is not in that situation.

Whose advice should he seek to check on this point? Each of the people he might turn to is potentially biased. This is not to deny that there are people who can take a detached view. But they are in a minority and are not easy to identify. With the best will in the world, most of the people with an interest in one of the ways of providing a pension will allow it to influence their judgement, in spite of their attempts to comply with the Financial Services Act and give 'best advice'.

An insurance broker may accurately choose which insurance company is likely to provide a better result than any other insurance company. A pensions consultant may cover a wider range of possibilities. But neither he nor an insurance broker will earn any commission by advising potential clients to stay where they are. A bank manager is very much aware (hopefully unconsciously) that his employer has an insurance subsidiary or department. And so on.

The position is not as hopeless as it seems. Some brokers and consultants are willing to put themselves in an unbiased position by agreeing to accept no reward from any provider of pensions they might recommend, if the client pays a fee for the advice. The amount of the fee is negotiable and depends on the amount of advice required.

Any employee who preferred not to pay a fee or could not afford it could seek advice from a number of brokers and consultants in competition with each other and from the manager of your pension scheme, if you have one, and compare what they tell him.

You are almost certainly in a stronger position. You are important to your existing financial advisers. They want to retain your confidence and support. They have an added incentive to ensure that you receive the best advice they can give.

1. What are the Choices?

'All human beings are born free and equal in dignity and rights' according to the Universal Declaration of Human Rights. But rights in relation to the provision of pensions do not arise until many years after birth. The Social Security Act 1986 has reduced the inequalities of those rights, as far as they relate to employees. In particular it has created the rights which concern this chapter.

SERPS

The state earnings related pension – SERPS, for short – is the addition which started to build up from 6 April 1978. (The flat rate state pension is what is still often referred to as the 'old age pension'.) Unless somebody takes action to alter an employee's situation, he automatically builds up an entitlement to a SERPS pension in respect of his earnings between certain limits. Therefore the source and security of that pension are important.

It may be helpful to start by dispelling one possible illusion. Reference is sometimes made to the National Insurance Fund. It is not surprising that some people imagine this is a money mountain built up over the years out of NI contributions in preparation for paying state pensions. Although some governments have set out to create such a source for pensions, their hopes have quickly foundered. Unexpected demands to counteract inflation for people who have already retired have quickly depleted the accumulating fund. The responsible minister has needed to ask periodically for further resources to be provided, in one way or another.

Another clarification of the system is also desirable. Although an employee's entitlement to a state basic retirement pension will depend, to some extent, on the number of years in which he has paid NI contributions, even the current year's total receipts from all such contributions is too small to pay all the benefits. The Treasury has to add a subsidy.

In the circumstances, it is not unusual for people in the pensions industry to say that NI contributions are just part of the UK tax system. They see them as resembling the fee which a motorist pays for a road fund licence which is not necessarily used to pay for building new roads and maintaining old ones.

To correct any mistaken ideas about the National Insurance Fund and to point out the need for NI contributions to be subsidised by the Treasury is not to suggest that payment of state pensions is an act of grace and may stop at any minute. The history of state pensions since they started in 1908 has been of continued payment to an increasing proportion of the population. However, it is right to remember that this year's state pensions, both flat rate and SERPS, come out of this year's receipts by the Government of NI contributions and other forms of taxation.

The law relating to state pensions has changed several times since they were introduced. The changes have given effect to the opinions of successive governments on how to relate the pensions to developments in the economic and political environment.

The 1975 Act provided for the SERPS pension to build up, between 1978 and 1998, to reach 25 per cent of an employee's average earnings between lower and upper earnings limits. (The limits are approximately 0.25 and 1.75 per cent of National Average Earnings. And each year's earnings of an employee, between those limits, are revalued to allow for inflation before the average is calculated.)

The 1986 Act is claimed to take due account not only of current conditions but also of what conditions are thought likely to be in 30 or 40 years' time. The changes which that Act makes will generally not affect people who start to draw SERPS pensions before 6 April 2000 but will reduce the amount of those pensions for people who qualify for them subsequently. The impact of the change will be small for those who reach pension age in the tax year 2000/1. It will be phased over ten years, so that only people who reach pension age after 5 April 2009 will suffer the full effect. For them, the SERPS pension will be 20 percent of the relevant earnings instead of 25 per cent.

Both the predicted changes in the ratio of pensioners to earners in the population and the way in which SERPS is being altered to take account of them are important. The former suggest that a future government may need to make further alterations: the latter offers hope that any such alterations will be phased-in instead of being imposed suddenly.

Contracting out or living on top

The simplest way for you to ensure that your employees will have larger retirement incomes than the state provides is to have your own pension scheme. Unless you use it to contract the members out of SERPS, they will have both their entitlement to flat rate and SERPS pensions and their entitlement under your own scheme. In the world of pensions, the jargon for this situation is that your scheme is 'living on top' of the state scheme.

Many employers arrange schemes in this way. Others prefer that their schemes should accept a commitment to provide pensions which take the place of SERPS. By doing this, they effectively receive a DHSS contribution to the cost of their schemes which approximates to the average cost of the SERPS pensions to which the members would otherwise be entitled.

Similar scope exists for employees who choose to have personal pensions to contract out of SERPS. Chapter 7 examines advantages and disadvantages of contracting out.

Employers' schemes

No private employer can safely promise that he will have sufficient profits many years hence to pay pensions to his present employees when they retire. This is partly why most employers who promise their employees pensions create pension funds. In one way or another, this ensures that money will be available to pay the pensions. Chapter 6 describes various ways of doing this, and Chapter 4 mentions the associated tax advantages.

Although the creation of a properly established and managed fund may remove any doubt that employees will receive pensions in due course, it does not guarantee that the fund will be large enough to provide pensions as large as the employer intended. Unforeseen circumstances may prevent the employer from contributing as much as he had expected. They may also prevent the fund from earning the interest and achieving the capital gains which had been thought likely. The next two subsections describe the two principal choices an employer can make in relation to future contribution commitments. Chapter 6 indicates how investment risks may be minimised, and the possible consequences of doing so.

Defined benefits

The majority of large schemes and many of the smaller ones calculate each member's pension by a formula relating pension to length of service and earnings at retirement, or slightly earlier. These are usually referred to as 'final salary schemes' or 'final pay schemes'.

In occupations which tend to provide larger earnings some years before retirement than subsequently, a different formula may be used. It takes account of a member's average earnings after revaluing each year's earnings in line with an index to take account of the effect of inflation. These schemes are, predictably, usually referred to as 'average pay schemes'. They are suitable not only for those manual workers whose physical powers diminish during their last few years of employment but also for such people as travelling salesmen whose mental or physical stamina may diminish similarly.

For both these types of defined benefits scheme, the eventual cost is unpredictable. If such a scheme is to provide such benefits, somebody must take on an open-ended commitment, promising to make sure that the fund is large enough come hell or high water. For practical purposes, that somebody is the employer. But it would be wrong to exaggerate the extent of his commitment. Choosing how large the contributions to the fund are to be is no hit-or-miss affair.

The basis of the contributions is decided after

receiving the recommendations of an actuary. This is a specialist mathematician whose training and experience enable him to make reasonable predictions of the cost of a pension scheme. He takes account of the likely investment yield of the pension fund; the ages of the members; how long, on average, they are likely to live; their current earnings and their likely pay increases.

To allow for differences between his assumptions and the progressive experience of the scheme, the actuary reviews its finances at intervals, usually every three years. If he considers it appropriate, he recommends an alteration to the contributions.

The actuary does not calculate the cost of providing the benefits under a final pay scheme for each member separately. If he did, everybody would be able to see that the cost of a member's pension rises steeply as he approaches retirement. The total cost of the additional amount of pension relating to each successive pay rise must be met in progressively fewer years.

In practice, contributions are calculated as a percentage of the total of all the members' earnings, irrespective of who is to pay them. Because the cost of each younger member's pension in a given year is proportionally less than the cost of each older member's future pension, the former's contributions are meeting part of the cost of the latter's pension. This would be immaterial if every young member remained with the employer until retirement and his final pay would be equivalent to what all his predecessors had received. In practice, many of the young members will leave the employment early, and some of those who stay will not achieve equivalent final pay.

Money purchase

To remove what is seen as an unfair cross-subsidy of the old by the young, many employers have chosen to adopt a different basis for their schemes. It is usually referred to as 'money purchase', but the Inland Revenue have coined the description 'defined contribution'. By this method of funding pensions, the contribution for each member is calculated either as a fixed amount or as a percentage of whatever part of his earnings is to be pensionable. For the purpose of building up a fund to pay for his pension, his contributions are segregated from the contributions of all the other members.

The segregation may amount to no more than a record-keeping exercise, but when a member reaches retirement the records show how large a sum the progressive investment of contributions made for him has realised. That sum is available to provide his pension.

In many schemes, a uniform percentage contribution is made for each member. In others, different percentages or level amounts apply to different members. They may be chosen by the employer, or by agreement between him and each member.

Some schemes have only one member. They are usually referred to as 'individual arrangements' and may be set up for such diverse situations as those of an employer who has only one employee and a large company whose managing director has accepted his appointment on the understanding that the basis of his pension will be far more generous than that for everybody else.

Hybrid schemes

High inflation during the 1970s made money purchase schemes unpopular, because retiring members found that their pensions bore little relation to their earnings immediately before retirement. The exception was those individual arrangements and small schemes for which progress was monitored year by year and contributions were increased to take account of the cost of living.

Worries about cross-subsidies between younger and older members of final pay schemes and dissatisfaction with the size of pensions which are preserved for early leavers have reawakened interest in money purchase. To quieten the fears of those members who fear the effects of a possible return of inflation, some employers have arranged schemes which operate on a money purchase basis but incorporate a final pay guarantee at retirement. These schemes, which understandably cost more than equivalent final pay schemes without a money purchase underpin, are sometimes known as 'hybrid schemes'.

Personal pensions

For the purposes of this book, personal pensions are the kind of pensions which the Social Security Act 1986 promised and the Finance (No 2) Act 1987 described in greater detail. They are acceptable as a means of contracting out of SERPS but can be arranged without any such intention.

Solo efforts

Apart from their eligibility for contracting out, personal pensions bear a marked resemblance to the retirement annuities which the Finance Act 1956 introduced for the self-employed and employees who did not belong to employers' pension schemes. These became familiar to many people as section 226 annuities, because the relevant part of the 1956 Act was consolidated into section 226 of the Income and Corporation Taxes Act 1970.

However, the Finance (No 2) Act 1987 not only made various alterations to the requirements of section 226 but also added to the list of classes of financial institution which could provide personal pensions. It also made section 226 inapplicable to new annuities for the self-employed.

Group schemes

Personal pensions are essentially contracts between individuals and the pension providers. Some of the providers think that there is a sound argument in favour of arranging a common communications system for several employees of one employer who want to fix up personal pensions with the same provider. It could achieve a saving in administrative expenses, and this might enable the provider to offer better terms to the group than to each of the individuals separately. The employer might even be willing to deduct each employee's contributions from his pay and make a bulk payment to the provider.

Different providers will doubtless develop different patterns for their group personal pension plans. The fundamental principle must still apply. Each member of a group is in a direct contractual relationship with the provider.

2. How Flexible are the Choices?

'Nothing is so certain as the unexpected', according to an old French proverb. So every employer and employee would be well advised to check on the scope which each available choice offers for coping with unforeseen circumstances.

An employee may discover that his choice is not the best he could have made. All will not be lost. He will have considerable scope for remedying the situation. But it must be emphasised that he is likely to suffer to some extent as a result of having headed in the wrong direction in the first place. His area of choice may be reduced, and he may have to pay for the work which his change of direction entails for somebody.

SERPS

The degree of flexibility offered by the state earnings related pension is less than that of the alternatives. The Government accepts that flexibility of retirement age is desirable and sought views on the subject in a Green Paper in June 1985. The White Paper which followed in December 1985 commented: 'Many of those who responded favoured greater flexibility; but none suggested a way of introducing the "decade of retirement" outlined in the Green Paper without substantial initial costs. The Government's aim remains that of increased flexibility. We will continue to examine possible ways of moving towards the decade of retirement.'

Meanwhile everybody's SERPS pension commences at the same time as his flat rate state pension. It cannot commence before the state pension age – 60 for women and 65 for men. It may start up to five years later. Indeed it may need to if the pensioner is still earning. If his earnings in any week exceed a given limit, his pension for that week will be reduced; if his earnings exceed the limit by quite a modest amount, the pension will be extinguished. The limit and the cut-off point are reviewed each time the state pension is increased.

At state pension age, someone who is entitled to a retirement pension may choose to defer its commencement. He may also choose to discontinue drawing it, subsequently, if this appears appropriate. But if payment recommences he cannot discontinue it again, ie discontinuance is permitted once only. If payment is deferred for more than six weeks, the amount of the pension is increased by 1/7 per cent for each week of deferment. Clearly deferment is logical for anybody who expects to have regular earnings which would largely or completely extinguish his state pension.

Five years after pension age, no further deferment is permissible, but the limit on earnings no longer applies. Women and men draw their state retirement pensions from 65 and 70, respectively, without any account being taken of any earnings they may have.

It may be desirable to mention that, although occupational pensions are generally regarded as deferred earnings and are taxable as earned income, receiving such a pension does not affect anyone's right to receive a state retirement pension. It may disentitle the pensioner to unemployment benefit.

Occupational pensions

The rules of a pension scheme may permit considerable flexibility regarding when a member starts to draw a pension and the form in which the benefits are paid. Where a scheme is used to contract out of SERPS, this flexibility relates only to benefits which are additional to certain minimum benefits the scheme must provide as a condition of contracting out. But it remains an important feature. Where a scheme lives on top of SERPS, flexibility exists across the board.

Foremost among the options which schemes traditionally include is that of taking a lump sum in place of part of the pension. The sum must not exceed an amount related to earnings by a formula laid down by the Inland Revenue. Subject to compliance with that formula, a scheme which was established before 17 March 1987 may be able to allow a member who joined the scheme before that date to take a lump sum in place of the whole of a moderately sizeable pension. The scope is considerably less for an employee whose membership of a scheme began on or after that date. However, a member who retires in such bad health that 'the expectation of life is unquestionably very short by comparison with the average for the same age and sex' may receive a lump sum in place of the whole of his pension, irrespective of the date on which he joined the scheme. The Appendix gives further details of the limitations on lump sums.

A member may also exchange part of his pension for a widow's or dependant's pension, to commence after his death. Although few members exercise this option, it can be very useful.

In contrast, many members exercise an option to retire on pension before their normal retirement age. Early retirement is usually allowed at any age on grounds of 'physical or mental deterioration which is bad enough to prevent the member from following his normal employment or which seriously impairs his earning capacity'. It may also be allowed within ten years of his normal retirement age, irrespective of his state of health. Although few people retire as early as that, many are glad to go two or three years early.

Another option is for a member to have the value of his pension transferred to an insurance company or friendly society of his choice which will pay an annuity larger than the pension the scheme would otherwise have provided.

In addition to being able to offer these kinds of flexibility, an occupational scheme can include benefits which do not feature in SERPS. It can provide pensions, both for members and their widows and dependants, which considerably exceed SERPS pensions. This is especially true in relation to members whose service started before April 1978 (when SERPS started). A scheme can also pay a substantial cash sum to dependants of a member who dies in service, and this is usually not subject to Inheritance Tax.

Personal pensions

As with an occupational pension scheme, the personal pension may permit considerable flexibility about when a pension is first drawn and the form in which its benefits are paid. Where a personal pension is used to contract out of SERPS, this flexibility relates only to benefits which are additional to the minimum benefits the arrangement must provide as a condition of contracting out. But it remains an important feature. Where the holder of a personal pension does not contract out of SERPS, flexibility exists across the board.

First there is the option of taking a lump sum in place of part of the pension. The lump sum must not exceed a quarter of the value of the pension when payment begins. In other words, if Frank Green's personal pension provider has £20,000 available to provide Frank with a pension when he retires, the maximum lump sum he can receive is £5000. The remaining £15,000 must be used to provide him with a pension.

There is also scope for exchanging part of the pension for a widow's or dependant's pension, to commence after the personal pensioner's death.

Payment of a personal pension may commence at any age between 50 and 75. It may commence sooner if the Inland Revenue are satisfied that the holder's occupation is one in which people customarily retire before 50. Early commencement is also acceptable on the grounds of the holder's 'becoming incapable through infirmity of body or mind of carrying on his own occupation or any occupation of a similar nature for which he is trained or fitted'.

Contributions for a personal pension may be made to any of a wide range of financial institutions, but when payment of the pension is due to commence the accumulated fund must be handed over to an insurance company or friendly society which will provide the pension. The pensioner may choose the insurance company or friendly society.

In addition to being able to offer these kinds of flexibility, a personal pension can include benefits beyond the range featured in SERPS. It can provide pensions, both for members and their widows and dependants, which considerably exceed SERPS pensions. It can also pay a substantial cash sum if the holder dies without attaining the age of 75. If no pension has become payable either before or because of his death, there can be a refund of contributions plus reasonable interest. It may be possible to arrange that those cash sums are not subject to Inheritance Tax.

Other flexibilities

The choice an employee makes between the three ways of providing a pension does not lock him into a situation he may come to regret. However, if he wishes to adopt a different route to his pension later, there may be fewer routes available.

If an employer has an occupational scheme for his employees, he has a right to say whether an employee who chooses not to join when he becomes eligible for membership or who leaves the scheme can apply to join later. Some pensions consultants suggest that an employee might reasonably be allowed to change his mind once, but that more frequent chopping and changing should not be available, as far as an occupational scheme is concerned. Because the employer is likely to find himself picking up the bill for switching, this appears to be sound advice.

The DHSS is more flexible, but if an employee wishes to switch from one contracted-out personal pension to another, the DHSS insists on making changes on 5 April. It can make minimum contributions to only one scheme in any tax year. Subject to that proviso, an employee can move from one contracted-out pension provider to another. He can also move into or out of SERPS.

Where contracting out is not an issue, moving from one personal pension provider to another is not difficult. The new provider is keen to welcome a new client. The old provider may be reluctant to see him go, but takes solace in the fee, levied in one way or another, to pay for the work involved.

3. Who Pays?

'You pays your money and you takes your choice.'

As far as the flat rate state pension is concerned, there is no room for argument about how much it is and who pays it. The DHSS pays it, and legislation lays down precisely how the employer and employee contribute to the cost and the basis of calculation of what each pensioner is to receive. But, other things being equal, the 1986 Act gives the employee a greater area of choice than the employer in relation to the source of other pension payments.

Both employer and employee must contribute to the cost of a pension for the employee, over and above the flat rate state pension, unless the employer voluntarily pays the employee's share for him. The employee automatically has scope for choosing how contributions made for him will be used to provide him with an additional pension; the employer can choose whether or not to widen that scope. Both parties can choose, within limits, whether they will contribute more than the law requires and if so, how much.

SERPS

Social Security legislation requires employees and employers to make what are called 'primary' and 'secondary' Class 1 National Insurance contributions respectively to the cost of state pensions. An employee who goes on earning after state pension age does not contribute after that age, but his employer's contributions must continue until the employment ceases.

Where an employee is contracted out of SERPS because of his membership of an occupational pension scheme, primary and secondary NI contributions are payable at reduced rates which exclude the cost of SERPS, *except in the circumstances to which the next paragraph refers*. Where he is contracted out by arranging a personal pension, the cost of SERPS is included in the NI contributions but the DHSS subsequently pays it to the provider of the personal pension.

A member of an occupational scheme which is not contracted out may himself be able to contract out by making free-standing additional voluntary contributions (FSAVCs). A procedure similar to that for a contracted-out personal pension applies. Full primary and secondary NI contributions are payable, and the DHSS makes a payment to whoever provides benefits in respect of the FSAVCs. *This facility is not available to a member of a simplified final salary scheme – see Chapter 4.*

Employers' schemes

For the purpose of this book, any pension arrangements an employer makes are assumed to be approved by the Inland Revenue, as described in the next chapter. Any which lack that approval are irrelevant.

With one exception, which we shall come to in a moment, an employer must always contribute to the cost of an occupational scheme, and his contribution must be more than a mere token amount. Some employers pay the whole of the cost of their schemes. For them, the only restriction on what they pay is that the benefits their contributions provide must not exceed the maximum amounts approvable by the IR.

An employer may make membership of his scheme conditional on each member's contributing to the cost on a defined basis. The contribution may be a flat amount which applies to each member. More often it is a percentage of each member's earnings or of a specified part of them.

Whether a member has to make such contributions or not, he may usually make voluntary contributions. Because these are additional to the normal contributions (whether the member makes any part of them or the employer alone contributes) it is common practice to refer to them as 'additional voluntary contributions' (AVCs).

Formerly the right to make AVCs depended on the rules of the scheme. It existed only if the rules said so. The 1986 Act opened the door for members of all schemes to make AVCs, unless there was a special reason which justified disallowing them. Such reasons are unlikely to feature often but it would clearly be unacceptable to permit AVCs to a scheme if the rules automatically provided the maximum benefits the IR would approve. Any AVC would then take the benefits beyond the limits.

The Finance (No 2) Act 1987 introduced another relaxation to encourage members to make AVCs. It permits the FSAVCs to which the previous section of this chapter refers. These are contributions to a scheme other than one to which the employer contributes. As long as the employer is contributing to at least one scheme to which a member belongs, the member may make AVCs to another scheme.

Finally it must be noted that the total contributions (other than NI contributions) which a member makes to pension schemes in relation to his employment (whether compulsorily or voluntarily) must not exceed 15 per cent of his earnings from that employment in any tax year.

There is one other source of contribution available to some employers' schemes. Where a scheme contracts out for the first time between 1 January 1986 and 5 April 1993, a special incentive payment will normally be available from the DHSS in respect of any member whose job has not previously been contracted out in another occupational scheme since 1 January 1986. Chapter 7 explains this more fully.

Personal pensions

If a personal pension is contracted out, there is no obligation for any contribution other than the minimum contribution to be made. The minimum contribution comes from the DHSS and generally equals the difference between the full rate primary and secondary NI contributions for the earner and the corresponding reduced rate NI contributions which would have been payable if he had been in a contracted-out occupational scheme.

Whether a personal pension is contracted out or not, the earner may contribute up to 17.5 per cent of his net relevant earnings in each tax year. (An employee's net relevant earnings are usually his earnings taxable by the PAYE system under Schedule E.) If he is at least 51 years old at the beginning of the tax year, he may contribute more than 17.5 per cent. The following are the appropriate limits:

Age on 6 April	Limit
51 to 55	20%
56 to 60	22.5%
61 or more	27.5%

An employer may contribute to a personal pension if he so wishes, provided that the sum of his and the employee's contributions does not exceed the appropriate limit shown in the previous paragraph.

It is unlikely that the majority of employees who arrange personal pensions will make contributions of the maximum permissible percentage of their earnings in any year, even if their employers assist. But where an employee is able and willing to pay more than the maximum in a particular year, there may be scope for him to do so. The Finance (No 2) Act 1987 permits payment of a contribution and relating it back to the previous year, if there is unused relief in respect of that year's earnings. The Act also gives scope for carrying forward unused belief for up to six years. Thanks to these provisions, an employee who has been unable to afford maximum contributions in earlier years but whose financial situation has improved may be able to catch up on what he has missed.

There is one other possible source of contribution to a personal pension. Where it is contracted out before 5 April 1993, a special incentive payment will normally be available from the DHSS. This does not apply when the earner has been contracted out in an employer's occupational scheme for at least two years and was entitled to remain so, but left it voluntarily after 5 April 1988 while still working for the same employer. Chapter 7 explains this more fully.

4. What Tax Angles are There?

According to an old proverb, 'There are only two evils from which no man can escape – death and the king's taxes'. Legislation can do little about the first of those evils, but successive Finance Acts have contained tax concessions relating to contributions to the cost of pensions, the accumulation of pension scheme funds and the payment of benefits by those schemes.

SERPS

Among the expenses of his business which an employer can offset against gross profit in calculating taxable profit is the cost of employing staff. That cost includes not only their remuneration but also the secondary Class 1 National Insurance contributions he has to make for them.

The employees are less fortunate. They cannot claim their primary NI contributions as expenses for tax purposes. But if they arrange personal pensions and use them to contract out of SERPS, the minimum contributions the DHSS makes take account of the fact that employees' NI contributions are paid from taxed income. In other words, the amount of the minimum contribution for an earner is the amount of his pre-tax earnings which is needed to pay the relevant part of his own NI contribution. For example, if George White's earnings between the lower and upper limits are £3000 a year, the part of the NI contribution which relates to contracting out is £174. Of this amount, £114 comes from his employers and £60 from George. If the standard rate of Income Tax is 25 per cent, George's share of the minimum contribution is increased by the tax he has suffered on the £60 to £80, ie £60 divided by 0.75 (100 per cent − 25 per cent), raising the total minimum contribution to £194.

Inland Revenue approval of other pension sources

For tax advantages in relation to occupational and personal pensions to be available, the sources of those pensions must have the approval of the Superannuation Funds Office of the Inland Revenue. The basis of SFO approval of occupational schemes was laid down by the Finance Act 1970. It has been modified by several subsequent Finance Acts, including the Finance (No 2) Act 1987, which also set the pattern for approval of personal pensions. (The relevant legislation up to and including that Act's contribution is consolidated in the Income and Corporation Taxes Act 1988.)

To achieve SFO approval, a scheme must also satisfy the requirements of the Occupational Pensions Board. This is a body established by the Social Security Act 1973 to perform certain functions in relation to pension schemes. Its members are appointed by the Secretary of State for Social Services and include representatives of employers and employees as well as pensions specialists. The OPB checks that the scheme rules meet certain requirements of that Act and of the Social Security Pensions Act 1975.

If a scheme is to be contracted out, the OPB also checks that the rules comply with statutory requirements and that procedures dealing with such matters as notifying and consulting with affected parties – especially the employees and their representatives – have been complied with, before granting a contracting-out certificate.

The legislation which governs the operations of the SFO and OPB is concerned with three main requirements, the first being the security of the funds. For occupational schemes, the key to this is the need for a scheme to be 'established under irrevocable trusts'. The trustees of the scheme must administer it in accordance with the scheme rules and trust law. Their legal ownership of the funds of the scheme is separate from their ownership of any other property. Highly importantly, it is separate from the employer's business, even if the employer is a trustee of the scheme. If that business should become insolvent, the creditors could not touch the scheme funds.

For a contracted-out scheme, the rule requirements also include a limitation on how the trustees may invest the fund, and the OPB requires periodical reports, in prescribed forms, on the progress of the scheme.

The second requirement for approval of a scheme is that it is recognised by employer and employees as being set up in good faith to provide relevant benefits. These may be briefly summarised as benefits for members at and during retirement, and for their dependants after the death of the members. The Appendix describes the benefits more fully.

Thirdly, it is required that neither the amounts of the benefits nor the contributions made and accumulated to provide them should be unreasonably large. Failure to observe the three requirements could be seen as removing any justification for granting the tax concessions which approved schemes enjoy.

For personal pensions, the same three requirements exist but the means of attaining them differ to some extent. Any provider of personal pensions inevitably wants to offer an appropriate scheme, ie a means of providing pensions which can receive minimum contributions from the DHSS for earners who want to contract out. To become 'appropriate' a scheme 'must have been established either under the provisions of a trust or by a deed poll, or have been set up in such a way that individual trusts or deeds poll are created for every member'. The object is to ensure that dependants have an enforceable right to obtain any benefits to which they may become entitled. There is also an obligation for reports to be sent to the OPB each year.

Section 21 of the Finance (No 2) Act 1987 laid down requirements which a personal pension scheme must meet before it could obtain SFO approval. Briefly, it must not provide benefits other than an annuity payable from an acceptable age; a lump sum when the annuity commences in place of not more than a quarter of the value of the annuity; an annuity of acceptable amount payable to the widow or another dependant of the earner after his death; a lump sum payable on the earner's death before age 75 and a refund of contributions plus reasonable interest payable on his death if no annuity has become payable to him or his widow or a dependant. Although contributions may be paid to and invested by a wider range of financial institutions, each annuity and each lump sum payable on an earner's death must be paid by an insurance company or a friendly society.

Section 32 of the Act met the third requirement by laying down maximum rates of contribution to a personal pension.

Tax relief on employer's contributions

An ordinary annual contribution by an employer to an exempt approved occupational scheme is allowable as a business expense in the year in which it is paid. Allowance for a special contribution may need to be spread over two or more years. If the total of all special contributions the employer pays to all occupational schemes in the year in which they are paid exceeds the larger of £20,000 and the total of all his ordinary annual contributions in that year, the allowance must be spread over at least two years but not more than five years.

Neither ordinary annual contributions nor special contributions are treated as additional remuneration of the members for tax purposes.

If a valuation of a scheme by an actuary discloses that the value of its assets exceeds the value of its liabilities by more than 5 per cent, steps must be taken to reduce the excess. This may be done by reducing contributions for up to five years and/or increasing the benefits provided by the scheme. To any extent to which the surplus is not reduced to 5 per cent by these methods, it must be returned to the employer and taxed at the rate of 40 per cent. Regulations prescribe how the actuary must carry out the valuation and what assumptions he may make.

Contributions by an employer to an employee's personal pension are allowable as a business expense in the year in which they are paid. They must not exceed any amount by which the maximum permissible contributions by the employee exceed his actual contributions. The employer's contributions are not taxable as additional remuneration of the employee.

Tax relief on employees' contributions

A member of an occupational scheme is entitled to have any ordinary contributions he makes treated as a Schedule E expense. The tax relief is given by what is known as a 'net pay arrangement'. When operating the PAYE system, the employer deducts the contribution from the employee's pay first, and calculates tax liability on the pay net of that deduction. For example, if John Smith's monthly pay is £1000 and his pension contribution is £30, his tax deduction is calculated on £1000 − £30, ie on £970.

Tax relief is similarly allowable on additional voluntary contributions. There was formerly a requirement that AVCs must be made on a fixed basis and maintained for at least five years or until earlier termination of employment, although the trustees could allow discontinuance in a case of severe financial hardship. That restriction has been removed. A member's contributions may now fluctuate as long as his total contributions neither exceed 15 per cent of his earnings in any tax year nor overfund the benefits being provided for him.

If an employee arranges a personal pension, he receives tax relief on his contributions in a similar way to relief on mortgage interest, ie he deducts the relief from his contribution and pays the net amount to the pension provider. The provider then claims the amount of the tax relief from the Inland Revenue.

Investment income and capital gains

Exempt approved occupational pension schemes and approved personal pension schemes qualify for tax concessions in relation to their investments. Interest and dividend payments are not taxable as income. Nor is capital gains tax payable on any disposal of investments. These concessions have been allowed to exempt approved schemes since the Finance Act 1970 became effective. The Finance (No 2) Act 1987 added equivalent sub-sections to provide similar concessions for any unit trusts established to provide appropriate personal pensions.

Taxation of benefits

State pensions, both flat rate and SERPS, are taxable as earned income. So are occupational and personal pensions. But whereas state pensions are paid gross, and any tax liability is dealt with separately, occupational pensions are payable net of tax by the PAYE system. In determining the coding for this purpose the Inland Revenue take into account the pensioner's state pension. Personal pensions are payable net of standard rate tax.

The lump sum which can be paid in place of part of any occupational or personal pension when payment of the pension is due is tax free. But if the trustees of an occupational scheme allow a member to receive a lump sum in place of the whole of his pension (when they are satisfied that he is in exceptionally bad health), the excess of the lump sum over what he could otherwise have received is taxable at the rate of 20 per cent. For example, Peter Brown could receive a lump sum of £1000 at retirement in place of part of his pension if he were in good health. But owing to his exceptionally bad health he can receive £3800 in place of the whole of his pension. Twenty per cent tax is payable on £3800 − £1000, ie on £2800.

Tax at the rate of 20 per cent is also payable on any refund of an employee's contributions which may be made to him if he leaves an occupational scheme before he has completed two years' membership.

The rules of an occupational scheme usually state that, if any lump sum is payable on the death of a member while in service − whether it is an insured benefit or a refund of contributions – the trustees have discretion as to which of several possible recipients will receive the lump sum. Where nobody receives the lump sum automatically on the death, there is no liability for Inheritance Tax. If an earner arranges for his benefits under a personal pension to be held by trustees of a separate trust outside the scheme, and those trustees are given comparable discretion in relation to death benefits, a similar result may be achieved.

5. Should an Employer Try to Influence Employees' Choices?

Andre Gide, the Nobel literature prizewinner said, 'We let ourselves be influenced by a woman or those whom we want to please, whose regard or esteem we want to win'. An employer's position may be ambivalent. Dare he let any influence he may have with employees who want to please him affect their decisions about retirement incomes? And how much blame may he attract from employees whose goodwill he wishes to cultivate if his retirement provision for them falls short of expectations?

Dangers of under- and over-involvement

Inertia can be a brake on progress. It can also save somebody from disaster if his only alternative to staying put is stepping onto a slippery slope. Many employees are unaware that they have a right to choose who will provide any pensions they receive, other than the flat rate state pension. Many others make no effort to discover what choices there are, or brush them aside as being irrelevant. Some are convinced that whatever the Government does must be bad, so any change must be a change for the worse.

In the circumstances, a caring employer is unlikely to contemplate doing nothing. Such an attitude leaves the field open for anybody with a vested interest in encouraging employees to make the choice he advocates.

That does not only mean a salesman. There are political and religious extremists with a mission to dissuade their fellows from acting in ways the majority of thinking people would favour or find acceptable. An employer who actively encourages his employees to 'exercise their democratic right to vote' and tries to present them with a simple, accurate and unbiased statement of their pension choices helps them to be more aware and less gullible.

Unless the statement is simple, it will have little or no impact with the people to whom it is addressed. Unless it is accurate and unbiased, it may lead to a comeback if it persuades somebody to take a line which experience shows to be ill-advised. Circulating misleading or inaccurate information could be held to constitute negligence if somebody acted on it and suffered a loss as a result. And if an employer gave biased information to encourage an employee to choose a personal pension with a particular financial institution, it is conceivable that the employer might be contravening the Financial Services Act.

The attitudes of younger and older employees

It is understandable that young people see retirement as a distant and relatively unimportant event by comparison with an impending marriage, birth or holiday. This year's expenses are very real whereas the possibility that essential living expenses in retirement may swallow and exceed every penny of pension is so 'iffy' as not to be worth worrying about. 'Sufficient unto the day is the evil thereof.'

So a young employee's thoughts may run on the lines, 'My pay packet is always too small, thanks to all the deductions. The cost of SERPS is unavoidable, but I'm certainly not paying a penny more.'

An older employee is more likely to want to know the alternatives. He has seen more of the difficulties his parents and other retired people experience. He may be willing to make additional voluntary contributions to his employer's pension scheme if somebody explains the tax advantages.

But generalisations can be misleading. Some young people are very far-sighted and take a keen interest in the advantages and disadvantages of various ways of providing for retirement. And some people who are nearing retirement are still waiting, like Mr Micawber, for something to turn up, but doing nothing about it.

The attitudes of some married women employees

Nearly half of the country's employees are not in pensionable employment. Many of them are part-time employees, a large proportion of whom are married women. That, in the eyes of many observers, may be seen as cause and effect. This explanation may be an accurate assessment, but there is little logic in the situation.

Many married women claim that they go out to work to make ends meet. The cost of bringing up a young family is more than their husbands earn. And when the young family starts to earn, marry and have other young families, the grandchildren need support. So long-term part-time employment is a long-term stop gap. The employee cannot afford to contribute to the cost of a pension. She needs the whole of her earnings for living expenses.

By this time, paid employment has become a habit.

It is likely to continue until the woman's husband retires, hopefully with a pension. At that point, the couple experience the transition from a two-pay-packet family to a one-pension family. The percentage drop in income is enormous. A timely word of warning by an employer, years earlier, would hardly have come amiss.

The attitudes of part-time employees

Not all part-time employees are married women. Some are people who are already drawing pensions, having retired from occupations with early retiring ages, such as the armed forces and the police. Again, they want to supplement their other sources of income. Although they have the prospect of adding the flat rate state pension to the pensions they are already drawing, they would be wise to think twice before passing up any offer of a second occupational pension.

Some of these part-time employees are what are colloquially known as 'moonlighters'. Understandably their second employers recognise the situation and see no need to think about providing pensions for people on the evening shift.

Times may change. The EEC plans to make the provisions of pensions for part-time employees compulsory, where full-time employees have a pension scheme. Do we always have to wait for progress to be compulsory?

Putting everybody in the picture

The Occupational Pension Schemes (Disclosure of Information) Regulations 1986 entitle members of occupational schemes to receive a considerable amount of information about their schemes. The regulations cannot ensure that the way in which trustees present the information is attractive or readable though. It is possible to comply with the regulations without making most of the members of a scheme any the wiser. Few of the people who drafted the regulations are likely to have given serious thought to the needs of scheme members who literally or metaphorically cannot read.

An astute employer wants his employees to know that what he pays for their scheme is providing them with valuable benefits. He wants value for his money. And a caring employer – who must surely also be an astute employer – wants his employees to know as much as possible about what a scheme will provide for them. He also wants them to know the possible significance of their freedom to choose whether to belong to the scheme, to supplement it or to follow another route to pension provision.

Telling them all this simply, informatively and in a way that makes them want to understand, is no easy task. Whoever designs the presentation must bear in mind that he has to teach people who know virtually nothing about pensions, and that many of them have a limited capacity for learning by reading. They need to hear the message, and to see it presented in a way they can understand. For a large scheme, spending a considerable sum on a first class video to achieve both these objectives may be a good investment. For the majority of schemes, a well illustrated talk by a competent speaker may give better value for money.

To say that the first requirement for a speaker is an ability to speak is not a facetious remark. A good speaker who knows nothing about the subject is preferable to an expert who is a poor speaker. The good speaker has the ability to familiarise himself adequately with any subject which his audience is capable of understanding. The expert may never acquire the ability to speak effectively.

The good speaker plans his talk in a logical

sequence which his audience will be able to follow and find ways to illustrate what he is going to say, both visually and verbally. He creates a presentation which will attract and hold the attention of his audience. He deals with questions sympathetically, and he senses when his answers leave a questioner puzzled. He makes an opportunity to speak to the questioner alone, later, so as to help him to grasp the important facts.

Arranging for the audience to break up into small discussion groups after a talk may consolidate what has been said and give scope for clarifying any difficult points. The smallness of the groups is important. It helps even shy people to speak, and reduces the fear of appearing stupid when experiencing difficulty in understanding what others might regard as simple ideas.

Inducements to belong to a scheme

An employer who already has an occupational scheme will usually be reluctant to see members leaving it and relying on SERPS or arranging personal pensions. The fact that he is contributing to the cost of the scheme is a bonus. It should influence members' thinking and is worthy of emphasis. But the structure of the scheme deserves careful thought. It may have been designed several years ago and need modifying to bring it into line with more modern practice. Skilled publicity for even small changes can increase loyalty to the scheme disproportionately to their cost.

An employer who has no scheme may increase his employees' loyalty to him by taking advantage of the facility for setting up a contracted-out money purchase scheme. The cost to him need not be enormous, but his payment of whatever contribution he makes to supplement the minimum contribution should receive good publicity. And the employees should be told how the scheme compares with the alternatives.

Because of the employer's need to consult with his employees and their representatives about contracting out, there must be a possibility that the majority of them may be against it, preferring the certainty of SERPS to the unpredictable amount of protected rights. If the employer agrees to go along with the majority decision and arrange an occupational scheme which will live on top of SERPS, the minority who would prefer to contract out need not be thwarted. The March 1988 Finance Bill includes provision for allowing a member of a scheme to contract out by means of a personal pension. The important qualification to bear in mind is that no contribution may be made to the personal pension except the DHSS minimum contribution.

Another employer may choose to arrange a group personal pension scheme, achieving more favourable terms for his employees than the provider would offer them individually, and possibly promising to make a modest contribution for anybody who joins the scheme. He should, of course, be careful to check on the investment record of the provider, in the hope that he will avoid the embarrassment of discovering, in later years, that one of his employees had achieved a better result by going to another provider, instead of accepting the favourable terms and the employer's contribution.

But when an employer is trying to help his employees to choose the best route to retirement pensions, he should not forget the needs of dependants of any employee who dies while still in service. It is permissible for an employee who arranges a personal pension to remain a member of an occupational scheme if no benefit is payable for him under the scheme except on his premature death. Some employers think it worthwhile to continue this provision for any member who arranges a personal pension, so as to ensure that there are no recriminations if a member omits to provide any protection for his dependants. Others prefer to make it clear to any employee who decides to leave the scheme and follow the personal pension route that protection for his dependants will cease immediately.

Finally, an employer has no obligation to allow an employee who leaves a scheme to rejoin it, later. Nor need he allow an employee who declines to join a new scheme when it is established to be admitted subsequently. In spite of this, some employers allow a second opportunity for membership and some are even more flexible. Others make it clear that nobody who leaves or declines to join will have another chance.

6. How Should Pension Funds be Invested?

Lord Macaulay wrote, 'We have heard it said that 5 per cent is the natural interest of money'. If that is true, we live in unnatural times. Trustees of pension funds are failing in their duty if they accept so low a return on their investments. They need a greater yield, but a safe yield.

There are many financial institutions available for investing funds to provide pensions for individuals or groups. The difference between what the most and least successful of them will achieve is likely to be substantial, but predicting which will be which is not easy. Who can give reliable advice?

The advice of a representative of any of the institutions will inevitably be biased. He has a duty to present his employer's contract in the best possible light. Even an independent financial adviser cannot guarantee that what he recommends will do better than all the alternatives. He will base his advice on what he knows about the market and how his experience suggests he should apply that knowledge to a prospective client's circumstances.

The purpose of this chapter is to help an employer to understand and assess whatever advice he receives.

It may also help him to offer a timely warning to any employee who appears to be taking a starry-eyed view of a personal pension salesman's promises.

The range of institutions and the contracts they offer varies from one type of pension to another. To simplify the presentation, the chapter deals with personal pensions first, and then mentions the different opportunities available to money purchase occupational schemes and defined benefits schemes, in that order.

Personal pensions

Accumulating a fund

The essence of a contract to provide a personal pension is that the contributions made by the earner (and by the employer and the DHSS, if they are contributing) will accumulate until the time comes for the earner to draw a pension. Then the amount which has accumulated must be used to pay for a pension for the earner (and possibly also a pension payable after the earner's death to a widow or another surviving dependant). Until retirement comes, the contributions may be paid to a bank, a building society, a unit trust or an insurance company or friendly society. When retirement arrives, the responsibility for any pension must be taken by an insurance company or a friendly society. Any other kind of provider must pay over the accumulated contributions to an insurance company or a friendly society. The earner may choose the company or society.

If the earner dies without having reached retirement, the accumulation must be used, to any extent to which the contributions come from the DHSS (or are any part of a transfer payment from another pension provider which relates to protected benefits or guaranteed minimum pensions), to provide a widow's pension. If there is nobody who qualifies for such a pension, a lump sum must be paid to someone nominated by the earner or to his estate.

Any other contributions may be used similarly, but the earner may wish to make more effective provision for dependants. This may be done by using part of his contributions to pay for life assurance cover for the period up to retirement, but no later than age 75.

With-profit policies

The way life assurance companies have conventionally provided the kind of personal pension which has been available for self-employed people since 1956 has been to issue what they call a 'with-profit policy'. This guarantees a basic amount of pension payable at a stated age, on top of which bonuses are added at intervals of one or three years, depending on the particular company. The amount of a bonus depends on how profitably and economically the company has invested its funds.

Some companies declare simple bonuses. This means that the amount of each bonus is based on the basic pension which the policy guarantees. An example will show how this works. John has a policy which provides a basic pension of £1000 a year. His insurance company declares bonuses every three years and has already added £200 to John's £1000. The company declares a further £7 per cent per annum. For three years this is a 21 per cent addition to the original £1000, ie £210. So the total pension, to date, is £1000 + £200 + £210 = £1410.

Other companies declare compound bonuses. This means that the amount of a bonus is based on the basic pension plus any existing bonuses. So if Robert's company declares compound bonuses every three years and has already added £200 to Robert's £1000 (making £1200 in all), a declaration of £7 per cent per annum will add 21 per cent to £1200 (making £1452 in all).

A company which declares compound bonuses is not necessarily more competitive than one which declares simple bonuses. So as to make an uncomplicated comparison of the ways in which simple and compound bonuses are added, the illustrations given in the last two paragraphs are both based on a bonus rate of £7 per cent per annum. In practice, if John's and Robert's companies had identical resources from which to declare bonuses, Robert's company would declare a lower rate than John's, so as to distribute the same total amount. (The longer-term policy holders would receive a proportionately larger share than the recent arrivals.)

Both simple and compound bonuses are sometimes described as 'reversionary bonuses'. This is jargon for saying that they are payable in the same way as the basic benefit. An imaginative policy holder has been known to call them 'revisionary bonuses' — which seems to be a more useful expression because it indicates that the bonuses revise the amount of benefit. It should be added that payment of a bonus, once it has been declared, is as much an obligation of the insurance company as payment of the basic pension.

Where a company declares bonuses every three years, it needs to make special provision for any policy holder who makes one or two years' contributions between the date of a bonus declaration and his retirement. The company deals with the situation by adding what is known as an 'interim bonus'. This may be at the same rate as the last reversionary bonus, or at a higher or lower rate. The rate depends on what the company considers will give the fairest treatment to all its policy holders, whether they are retiring or going on contributing.

How Should Pension Funds be Invested?

There is one other kind of bonus which figures in many companies' systems. This is a 'terminal bonus', added when the policy holder retires. Theoretically it makes an allowance for capital gains which have been built up during the period since the policy started but which have not been realised by selling the relevant investments. In practice, this may not be the source, but when a policy holder receives such a bonus he is not concerned about precisely where it came from.

For the 1988 generation of personal pensions, some companies have continued the conventional style of bonus. Some have devised with-profit systems which combine elements of the conventional style with elements of other insurance company methods which this chapter mentions later.

Before considering these other methods, we need to look at what is, effectively, a variation of the kind of policy at which we have been looking. In insurance jargon, we have been looking at a 'deferred annuity', and the variation is a 'pure endowment'. Instead of providing a basic pension (or annuity), and adding bonuses to it, a pure endowment provides a basic lump sum, adds bonuses to it, and converts it into a pension when the policy holder retires.

Both the deferred annuity and the pure endowment must allow the policy holder to have the value of the policy transferred to another insurance company at retirement. He is likely to use this facility if the other company will provide a larger pension. A deferred annuity provides a pension with company A which can be converted into a lump sum to buy a pension from another insurance company. A pure endowment provides a lump sum with company B which must be used to provide a pension with company B or with another company.

The method of providing personal pensions which we have been looking at relates essentially to life assurance companies and friendly societies. There are other ways in which such institutions may make provision. We shall look at them after the next two sections of this chapter.

Deposit accounts

The most readily understood way of accumulating a lump sum is to pay money into a deposit account, to which interest is added at regular intervals. The progress of the account is clearly seen from periodical statements.

Accounts which banks and building societies operate in connection with personal pensions have two advantages over their other deposit accounts. The first is that the interest credited to them does not need to have any tax deducted from it. The second is that the depositors cannot withdraw their money and spend it, although they have the right to have it transferred to another provider. But the deposits will usually be made for relatively long periods, and the holders of the deposits should be able to credit a higher rate of interest than for ordinary deposit accounts.

When a depositor reaches retirement, a bank or building society cannot pay the pension. It transfers the amount of the account to a life assurance company or friendly society for this purpose. The depositor has a right to choose the company or society.

Unit trusts

Another way of building up a fund to pay for a personal pension is by putting the contributions into a unit trust created exclusively for personal pensions. The managers invest the contributions in a range of securities, and whenever they receive interest or dividends on the securities, they invest the income in additional securities. The value of each participant's stake in the trust is measured in units, similarly to the way in which ordinary unit trusts operate.

Regulations made under the terms of the 1986 Act lay down certain restrictions on the way the managers of a trust may invest the fund. As long as they comply with those regulations, they may operate two or more trusts for personal pensions, including a greater proportion of speculative investments in one trust than in another. This will enable them to attract contributions from both cautious and adventurous earners.

When a participant reaches retirement, the managers of the trust cannot pay a pension. They must transfer the value of the units to a life assurance company or friendly society to do this. Again, the participant has a right to choose the company or society.

Other insurance methods

Some of the traditional providers of personal pensions measure their liability to a policy holder in a way similar to the deposit accounts of banks and building societies. They call this look-alike method 'deposit administration'. It was adopted so as to show more clearly than by longer-established methods the way in which a policy holder's contributions are used to provide benefits.

Another way of measuring a policy holder's rights is by means of a unit-linked policy. Instead of having a deposit account, kept in monetary terms, he is allocated units in an investment fund. The way in which the value of the units varies is similar to that in a unit trust.

Each of these types of policy gives a life assurance company or friendly society a more open way of dealing with the expenses which it incurs in the process of receiving, recording and investing contributions, and the cost of advertising and other ways of persuading potential customers (or members) to open an account. in the traditional types of policy, the impact of the expenses is hidden, the policy holder knowing only how much he pays and what benefits he receives. Deposit administration and unit-linked policies give some indication of how expenses are recouped, including the especially heavy initial expenses.

For deposit administration, the method may entail making a deduction from contributions before crediting them to an account; or levying a charge on the account; or adding a lower rate of interest than would be possible if a charge for expenses were made. To recoup initial expenses, higher charges may be made or lower interest added to the first year or two's premiums than to subsquent premiums.

For unit-linking, it is common to have two sets of units, which may be designated by such labels as 'ordinary' and 'special'. The management charges are heavier for special units than for ordinary units, and special units are allocated in respect of the first year or two's premiums, to recoup initial expenses. Ordinary units are allocated for subsequent years' premiums.

When the holder of a deposit administration or unit-linked policy reaches retirement, the company uses the value of the deposit account or units to pay for a pension. Both deposit administration and unit-linked policies include an option for a policy holder to have the value of the policy transferred to another company at retirement.

Guarantees cost money

When the holder of a personal pension reaches retirement, the provider has to honour the contractual obligations. If those depend on a unit trust or a unit-linked policy, the amount of the obligations is determined by the value of the underlying securities.

The provider has no problem about meeting the obligations. A sale of securities would provide the cash, if it was not immediately available from contributions recently received from other personal pension policy holders.

A provider who guarantees payment of a specific amount has to hold reserves which will be sufficient to meet that obligation, even if payment becomes due at a time when the prices of securities are low. He must create those reserves from the contributions received and the interest and dividends they earn. The obligation applies not only to the basic pension or pure endowment sum assured, from commencement, but also to reversionary bonuses from when they are added. A guarantee also applies to a deposit account, but this starts in a very small way with the amount of the first contribution less any management charge. The creation of reserves reduces the amount available to provide benefits but it ensures that the holder can rely on receiving the benefits he has been promised.

Gambles can lose money

The holder of a personal pension which depends on unit prices takes a chance that, although the value of units will tend to rise owing to the progressive investment of interest and dividends from the underlying securities, unit prices can and do fall, at times, in line with the prices of those securities. There are regulations which govern the ways managers of unit trusts can invest the funds for which they are responsible. While this reduces the risk of disastrous falls in unit prices it does not eliminate the likelihood that some people will receive pensions which are considerably smaller than they expected. That is a risk which anybody who chooses the unit trust or unit-linked policy route must accept.

Hedging bets

A speculative approach to a personal pension may provide a better income in retirement than any of the alternatives, but it would be unfortunate if the earner reached retirement at a time when the prices of the underlying securities were low. Because of this, many people prefer to put their money in an unexciting contract which guarantees the major part of the pensions they will receive.

There is no need for an earner to commit himself irrevocably either to being ultra cautious or to taking a gamble. Some providers of personal pensions offer scope for changing course at suitable times. In the most flexible contracts, switching is available not only between funds in a unit-linked contract but also between such funds and deposit administration and conventional with-profit systems, all available within a single contract.

Even where there is no such flexibility within the terms of a contract, the earner can stop contributing to it and start contributing elsewhere. He can normally also arrange for a transfer of the accumulated value of the contributions he has already made from the provider who holds them to another provider. Switching in this way may be more expensive than switching between different accumulation facilities of the same provider, but it is better than staying with a contract which is performing badly.

Taking advantage of the availability of switching facilities, an earner might start by choosing a unit trust or unit-linked contract which included speculative securities, and continue on that line until a few years from retirement. Choosing a moment at which the values of stock exchange investments were high, he might switch the source of his pension to less speculative units, or to a deposit account or a conventional insured contract. By doing this he might deprive himself of some of the additional investment income which he would have received if he had stayed put, but would not suffer if the price of the speculative units dropped.

Another way of hedging bets is for the earner to arrange for his contributions to be allocated to two or more methods of accumulation. For example, he might have the DHSS rebate invested very safely in a way which guaranteed that it would buy substantially (but not excitingly) more than the original rebates. Having secured that, the rebates would provide him with a predictable pension, he might put any additional contributions he could afford into speculative units. If he did happen to retire at an unfortunate time from the viewpoint of the investment market, he would still have a useful pension from the first source. It would ensure that the extent to which the remainder of his pension fell short of expectations did not ruin his retirement.

Money purchase occupational schemes

Many insurance companies offer policies to meet the needs of money purchase schemes for any number of members, from one upwards. The facilities which some of the companies offer are very similar to those which they offer for personal pensions. This is hardly surprising, because personal pensions operate essentially on a money purchase basis.

However, not all money purchase occupational schemes are backed by insurance policies. It is logical for any large scheme to be self-administered, irrespective of its basis of contributions and benefits.

Self-administered occupational schemes
Very large schemes

The funds of the largest pension schemes exceed those of many insurance companies. The investing of each of those funds requires the attention of a specialist department staffed by people experienced in analysing the potential of securities and dealing in various sections of the investment market. The investment manager of such a fund agrees an investment strategy with the trustees, and periodically reviews it with them so that they may make any adjustments which changes in the economic climate or in the structure of the scheme suggest or dictate. He delegates the implementation of various parts of the strategy to members of his staff who specialise in handling the relevant types of investment. Each of them may, in turn, supervise a group of people who handle routine and more imaginative aspects of acquiring and disposing of investments.

Relatively few funds require so large an investment team. Many more rely on an investment manager to supervise each transaction himself, taking the initiative in each deal, before delegating the paperwork to a secretary or a clerk. He may even involve himself in such routine work if planning and effecting sales and purchases does not occupy the whole of his working day.

His job description may include other responsibilities in addition to managing the investments. He may be the pension fund manager, concerned not only with investment work, but also with the recording of details of new entrants to his pension scheme, the calculation and payment of benefits for members who are retiring, and many other duties.

Shared specialists

If the size of a pension fund is too small to occupy an investment specialist full-time or to justify paying the salary of so valuable a person, the trustees may be reluctant to entrust the investments to somebody with a more general but shallower knowledge of pension fund management. They may arrange, instead, to share the time and cost of an investment specialist with one or two other pension funds.

Segregated managed funds

Another way of providing skilled management of the investments of a pension fund is to delegate the work to the investment department of such a financial institution as a merchant bank or an insurance company. In return for payment of a fee, the institution provides the services of an individual or a team to handle the investment of the fund as part of the day's work. The institution keeps the assets of the fund entirely separate from all other investments, but the staff who handle the fund bring to its management the skill and knowledge which they acquire during the course of the rest of their duties.

There is no clearly defined boundary between funds which need the control of a part-time (or even full-time) investment manager and those which should be handled by an outside financial institution. A manager has a more direct interest in his fund, but the scope which the staff of a financial institution have for consultation with one another may give them a more comprehensive grasp of investment opportunities than an individual manager would have.

Pooled managed funds

There is a way by which a fund considered too small for segregated management can enjoy the advantages of top class investment skill and a wide spread of investments. Merchant banks and life assurance companies offer pooled managed funds which provide such advantages for small pension schemes just as unit trusts do for private investors.

The managers of a pooled fund use the money they receive from scheme trustees to buy a wide range of investments. The pooled resources are together large enough to enable the managers to buy a balanced portfolio of investments. Each scheme's stake in the fund relates to its proportion of the total resources of the fund. The managers measure it in units, adjusting the total number of units in existence each month and allocating them to take account of sums invested and disinvested and the associated expenses, and to reflect fairly not only the sums each scheme has contributed but also the dates on which they were contributed.

Some financial institutions operate several pooled managed funds. An institution may offer a choice of, say, an equity fund, a gilt edged fund, a property fund, a Far Eastern fund and an Americas fund, plus a composite fund which is the managers' preferred combination of units in the other funds.

Some trustees prefer to choose the proportions of investment in the various funds they consider best for their scheme. They may consult their actuary before making each choice. He may advise them how best they may match the scheme's liabilities. If neither they nor the actuary doubts the wisdom of such a course of action, the trustees may decide to rely on the managers' preferred combination.

Whatever investment decision the actuary may recommend, there is one precaution which he will point to as essential where a scheme has a relatively small membership – perhaps fewer than 100. The fund could suffer severely or even disappear if there were several early deaths among the members.

Prudence dictates that the trustees should lay off the risk with an insurance company by effecting a group life assurance policy. The actuary may also recommend that the trustees should allow for the risk that too many pensioners might live to a great age, by purchasing annuities from an insurance company when members retire.

Insured defined benefits schemes

Many employers prefer to entrust the running of their pension schemes to pensions departments of insurance companies. Where a scheme is required for a small number of employees only, this can be a highly satisfactory arrangement. Opinions differ as to what constitutes 'a small number of employees' in this context. There are insured group schemes for as few as five employees and for as many as 500.

The insurance company usually takes care not only of building up a fund to provide retirement benefits but also of insuring benefits for dependants, which will be payable when members die while still employed, and setting up annuities to provide the pensions for retired members. (Sometimes a pensions consultant places the insurance of death benefits with a different insurance company.)

The accumulating fund to pay for the retirement benefits is usually guaranteed, to a substantial extent. Some companies operate it in money terms, similar to the deposit administration system described earlier in this chapter in relation to personal pensions: periodical additions of 'interest' measure the extent of the insurance company's increasing guarantee. Others create a pool of annuity credit which is used to provide the pensions of members as they reach retirement, periodical bonuses in the form of additional credit marking the increasing guarantee.

Whichever method the insurance company adopts

for showing the progress of the scheme, the basis of insured group defined benefits schemes is that the insurance company periodically reviews the adequacy of the fund. After calculating the value of the fund and the immediate and future liabilities, the company recommends to the trustees what future contributions should be made to the fund, on the basis of certain stated assumptions about investment conditions, salaries, staff turnover and mortality.

If the scheme were not insured, the trustees would arrange for an actuary to carry out the review and make the recommendations. The ability of the trustees of a defined benefits scheme to pay all the retirement benefits as they become due depends on their receiving and adopting sound recommendations, either from an insurance company or from an independent actuary. The difference between an insured scheme and a self-administered scheme is that the amount of the accrued fund under an insured scheme is guaranteed – a guarantee for which the trustees pay.

Comparing providers

Before arranging a personal pension, an employee should be confident that he is making a wise choice of provider, and before establishing an occupational pension scheme, an employer should be equally confident about how its investments will be managed. Each may ask a financial adviser for a recommendation.

It is important that he should know the enquirer's views on the desirable degree of caution. The adviser could be asked to put forward three choices, each offering a different scenario, and to make a comparison between their features. These should include their investment track records, their administrative reliability, and their charges, not only at the outset and at intervals subsequently, but also if money is switched within their funds or away from them. It is vital to know all the adverse features as well the favourable ones before making a choice.

The adviser should also be asked whether he charges a fee for his advice, or whether he receives commission or some other form of remuneration from whichever of his recommended financial institutions is chosen.

7. Should One Contract Out?

'A fair exchange is no robbery'. But does contracting out of SERPS provide a fair exchange? The answer depends on many factors. An advantage may lie sometimes with the employer, sometimes with the employee and sometimes with the taxpayer.

There is general agreement that contracting out may be profitable in relation to young employees but not at the other end of the age scale. Where to draw the dividing line depends not only on the sex of an employee but also on the uncertainty of future contracting-out terms and investment opportunities.

Possible routes to contracting out

When the Social Security Pensions Act 1975 established the state earnings related pension it also provided a basis for contracting out by means of a defined benefits occupational scheme. The rules of the scheme needed to include two criteria for benefits. The first was called 'requisite benefits', calculated by a formula chosen to suit the particular scheme but acceptable to the Occupational Pensions Board. The second was called 'guaranteed minimum pensions' (GMPs), determined by a formula laid down by the legislation which made them approximately equal to SERPS pensions.

Amending legislation removed the need for an acceptable requisite benefits formula. The only remaining adequacy requirement is that benefits must not be less than GMPs. In practice the benefits which most schemes provide normally comfortably exceed GMPs.

To any extent to which a GMP relates to employment before 6 April 1988, the DHSS is responsible for inflation-proofing it while it is in course of payment. The occupational scheme is responsible for inflation-proofing it to any extent to which it relates to employment on and after that date, except that the DHSS is responsible for covering any inflation in excess of 3 per cent per annum.

Since 1978, the advantage gained by replacing SERPS benefits by contracted-out defined benefits schemes has been that employer and employee make smaller National Insurance contributions. The reduction during the financial years between 6 April 1988 and 5 April 1993 is 5.8 per cent of earnings between the lower and upper limits – 3.8 per cent for the employer and 2 per cent for the employee.

Contracting out is now also permissible for money purchase schemes. To qualify they must have contributions at least as great as the reduction in the NI contributions. The reduction is referred to as the 'rebate' and that part of the scheme contributions must provide 'protected rights'. These comprise:

- a pension for each employee from state pension age
- a pension half as large for his widow if the employee dies in retirement
- a pension for his widow if the employee dies before retirement and the widow is over 45 or has dependent children.

(For a female employee, references to a widow must be taken to mean a widower.) The amounts of the protected rights depend on the size of the fund created by investing the rebate. They may be larger or smaller than SERPS would have provided.

An employee who does not belong to an occupational scheme may use an appropriate personal pension to contract out of SERPS. The system resembles that for a contracted-out money purchase scheme except that reduced NI contributions are not payable. Instead, the DHSS receives full NI contributions and pays the rebate to the personal pension provider. The provider will not receive the rebate until the end of the financial year to which the contributions relate. On the average, the rebate will probably reach the provider eight to ten months after the contributions are made. The provider will be unable to invest the rebate until he receives it.

Clause 53 of the March 1988 Finance Bill contains a further choice. An employee who belongs to an occupational scheme which **is not** contracted out may arrange a personal pension which **is** contracted out. But the only contribution to the personal pension which will be permitted will be the rebate.

Larger contributions may reduce expenses

In simple terms, it is true to say that receiving a contribution of £1000 a year involves a provider in the same administrative expense as receiving a contribution of £1 a year. The statement needs modifying in relation to a contracted-out personal pension, because part of the contribution comes from the earner and part from the DHSS. But whereas most earners want to make their contributions monthly, the DHSS pays the NI rebate once a year. The extra work entailed in crediting the rebate to the earner's account with the provider is small, but the additional amount available for investment may be substantial. If this induces a provider to offer more favourable terms for personal pensions to earners for whom larger contributions are payable, the inclusion of an NI rebate may be an important consideration in favour of contracting out.

There is another situation in which the inclusion or non-inclusion of the rebate may play a vital part in any argument about what action an earner ought to take in connection with the chance to arrange a personal pension. If he does not belong to a scheme and the amount he could afford to contribute to a personal pension is small, it may be less than the minimum amount which a provider would accept. The addition of the rebate might enable him to surmount that obstacle.

The five-year initial boost

The Government are encouraging contracting out by making an incentive payment for:

- any scheme which is contracted out for the first time between 6 April 1988 and 5 April 1993, and
- any personal pension, unless the earner has been for two years or more in an employer's scheme which is contracted out and he was entitled to remain a member but left it voluntarily after 5 April 1988, while still working for the same employer.

The incentive payment will be payable until 5 April 1993 and will be 2 per cent of earnings between the lower and upper earnings limits, or £1 a week if that is greater than the 2 per cent.

Changing pension providers

An employee who belongs to a contracted-out occupational scheme and changes his job after not less than two years can have a transfer payment made by that scheme to a new employer's scheme, or to a personal pension, or to a policy issued to him by an insurance company. If he leaves his employer's scheme but does not change his job, he may have a transfer payment made to a personal pension. A transfer payment is an amount of equal value to the rights which the employee accumulated in the scheme.

If a new scheme or personal pension is not contracted out, the old scheme can either retain the GMP or protected rights liability or – if the old scheme is a defined benefits scheme – pay a transfer premium to the DHSS which will then take over that liability. The transfer value will be reduced by the cost of retaining the liability or the amount of the transfer premium. Payment of such a premium is the most likely course of action.

If an employee leaves without having completed two years' scheme membership, GMP or protected rights must still be provided. He will also usually receive a refund of his contributions, minus his share of the cost of that provision. Tax at the rate of 20 per cent will be deducted from the refund. But an employer may treat members who leave within two years of joining the scheme on the same basis as members who complete that qualifying period.

A note of caution

When SERPS started in 1978, a scheme which was contracted out had to provide benefits which included a GMP approximately equal to what SERPS would otherwise provide. The basis on which a money purchase scheme or a personal pension can be contracted out is that the rebate and any incentive payment from the DHSS must be invested in an approved way to provide protected rights.

It must be emphasised that, although the protected rights may be larger than SERPS would provide, they may be considerably smaller. The eventual value of the rights will depend on the rates of rebate which successive governments authorise and the profitability of the investments the provider makes. Rates of rebate are reviewed every five years.

8. What Choice Will You Make?

(Checklists for employers)

'The wind of change is blowing,' though not in the way that the late Lord Stockton meant when he said those words. The wind is blowing through the world of pensions. It is changing the landscape; it is changing SERPS and occupational schemes; it is adding personal pensions and free-standing additional voluntary contributions to the range of pension-building facilities; it is increasing the scope for contracting out and for choosing where one's retirement income will come from. The number of pension providers is increasing, and so is the number of methods some of the providers offer for accumulating a fund. No employer can afford to ignore all this, and no caring employer will want to.

The decisions an employer makes about the extent to which he will make retirement benefits available to his employees will determine the adequacy of what some of them (and their dependants) will receive. The effectiveness with which he makes available information about his employees' scope for choice will have an important bearing on how many of them give careful and reasonable thought to what choice they should make.

To help employers plan their response to the wind of change, the remainder of this chapter consists of a series of checklists. They are intended as triggers to help an employer give constructive thought to how best to ensure his employees have the right environment in which to choose the source of their retirement income.

Checks on occupational scheme provisions

1. Is there an occupational scheme?
2. If 'yes',

    (a) is its basis final pay, money purchase or hybrid?
    (b) do members who leave service complain about what the scheme provides for them?
    (c) is it contributory or non-contributory?
    (d) do members appreciate how much the employer contributes?
    (e) do they complain about any contribution they have to make?
    (f) is the scheme contracted out?
    (g) should it be?
    (h) when was it last amended, otherwise than to comply with a change in the law?
    (j) is it generally acceptable to the employees?
    (k) if not, what complaints are there about it?
    (l) does it exclude any employees who might be included?
    (m) in the light of the answers to those questions, is it appropriate to revise the scheme basis?
    (n) if 'yes,' should the change affect:
    - retirement benefits?
    - death benefits?
    - employees' contributions?
    - contracting out?
3. If there is no occupational scheme,

What Choice Will You Make?

(a) have employees ever asked for one?
(b) has the employer considered starting one?
(c) if 'yes', why didn't he go ahead?
(d) in view of those answers and the new freedom for employees, would it be a good idea to install a scheme?
(e) if 'yes', should its basis be final pay, money purchase or hybrid?
(f) should it be contributory or non-contributory?
(g) should it be contracted out?
(h) would it be better to arrange a group personal pension scheme?
(j) would it be easier to answers questions (f) – (h) if the employer had quotations from competing advisers?
(k) from which of the following could the employer obtain advice on whom to consult
- his bank?
- his insurance broker?
- his accountant?

Checks on possible treatment of employees who leave an employer's scheme or refuse to join one

1. Should the scheme continue to provide protection for widows and dependants of employees who die while in the employment?
2. Should the employer warn leavers and non-joiners that they will be

    (a) debarred from future entry to the scheme?
    (b) eligible for later entry once only?
    (c) subject to special terms on any later entry?

3. Should the employer encourage them to arrange a personal pension by offering to contribute to it?

Checks on effectiveness of communication with employees

1. Will the employer:

    (a) leave employees to discover their new freedom?
    (b) give them the short DHSS leaflet (NP40)?
    (c) give them the longer DHSS leaflet (NP41)?
    (d) give them also a written summary of his occupational scheme intentions?
    (e) hire a video presentation about employees' pensions freedom?
    (f) arrange for somebody to address a meeting explaining the situation?
    (g) arrange for discussion groups to consolidate the information?

Appendix

Summary of the Principal Inland Revenue Limits on Benefits Under Occupational Pension Schemes – Except on Leaving Service

Note
1. This summary is a broad guide and is not exhaustive.
2. If a member belongs to two or more schemes in relation to the same employment, the benefits from those schemes must be added together when applying the limits.
3. The summary does not describe the simplified bases of approval of defined benefits and defined contribution schemes which were introduced in 1987 and the terms of which must usually be less generous than those in this summary.

Introduction

The size of the benefits which a scheme may provide depends principally on a member's earnings and the length of his service with the employer who has paid those earnings. For some company directors and former directors, and for members whose earnings have exceeded £100,000 in 1987/8 or any subsequent year, some of the limits are more restrictive. Details are omitted from this summary because those people are unlikely to be concerned with the possibility of arranging personal pensions.

Final remuneration

Limitations on benefits are defined by reference to what the IR refer to as 'final remuneration'. For the majority of members this may be calculated by whichever of two formulae gives the larger amount. They are:

(a) basic earnings in any one of the five years preceding normal retirement date (NRD) plus an average of fluctuating earnings during that year and the immediately preceding two or more years, and

(b) the average of total earnings during a period of three or more consecutive years which ended not earlier than ten years before NRD.

In relation to benefits payable on a member's death while in service, the same criteria are available, with the substitution of the date of death for NRD. Other criteria are also available and may produce a larger result. They are:

(c) the member's basic salary at the date of death plus the average of fluctuating earnings during the three years up to the date of death, and

(d) the total earnings in any period of 12 months ending not more than 36 months before the date of death.

Appendix

Retirement benefits

Table B1 shows the maximum pension which a member who joined the relevant scheme before 17 March 1987 may receive at his NRD, from all schemes of his current employer, or to which the employer has contributed, other than a scheme of National Insurance, if the member has retained no pension rights from an earlier occupation.

Table B2 shows the maximum lump sum for which the member may commute part (or the whole) of his pension, if he has retained no rights to a lump sum from an earlier occupation. Some schemes specifically provide lump sums and pensions, the latter being limited in accordance with the words in brackets in the heading to the second column of Table B1.

Members who joined a scheme on or after 17 March 1987 cannot have a pension of 40/60ths of final remuneration unless they complete at least 20 years of service by NRD. For shorter periods the maximum approvable is 1/30th of final remuneration for each year of service. And members who joined on or after that date cannot have a lump sum on the basis of Table B2 unless they are provided with maximum total benefits in accordance with the previous paragraph.

Revaluation of earnings

To allow for inflation, earnings for periods more than 12 months earlier than the date of retirement or death may be revalued in line with the Retail Prices Index (or another suitable index approved by the IR). There is an important proviso. In calculating the maximum lump sum which a member may receive at retirement, his earnings may be revalued only to any extent to which his total pension, including the pension equivalent of the lump sum, is based on earnings similarly revalued.

Table B1

Years of service to normal retirement date	Maximum pension (*including pension equivalent of any lump sum*) as a fraction of final remuneration
1-5	1/60th for each year
6	8/60ths
7	16/60ths
8	24/60ths
9	32/60ths
10 or more	40/60ths

Fractions of a year may be interpolated into the table.

Table B2

Years of service to normal retirement date	Maximum lump sum as a fraction of final remuneration
1-8	3/80ths for each year
9	30/80ths
10	36/80ths
11	42/80ths
12	48/80ths
13	54/80ths
14	63/80ths
15	72/80ths
16	81/80ths
17	90/80ths
18	99/80ths
19	108/80ths
20 or more	120/80ths

Fractions of a year may be interpolated into the table.

Example of revaluation of earnings

Daniel Peterson's final remuneration, based on actual earnings, is £18,000 per annum. If the relevant

Appendix

earnings were revalued in line with the Retail Prices Index, the equivalent final remuneration would be £24,000.

Because he has completed more than 20 years' service, IR limits would allow him to have a pension of 40/60ths if £24,000, ie £16,000 per annum, and to commute part of it for a lump sum of 120/80ths, ie £36,000. However, if his scheme can afford to provide him with a pension of £15,000 per annum only, the maximum lump sum Daniel can receive must be reduced in proportion, ie to £33,750.

Retained benefits from earlier employments

The IR designed the scales of maximum benefits in Tables B1 and B2 to enable a job-changer with no pension rights from earlier employments to achieve maximum benefits from his final employment, even if he serves in it for substantially less than the 40 years which the IR regards as a normal working lifetime.

For any member of a scheme who has retained a right to receive a pension and/or a lump sum at retirement on account of his previous employment, the IR imposes limitations on benefits otherwise permitted by Tables B1 and B2. The member's aggregate pension from all schemes must not exceed two-thirds of his final remuneration and his aggregate lump sum must not exceed one-and-a-half times final remuneration. For this purpose, benefits under a self-employed pension policy arranged during earlier self-employment or during non-pensionable employment are retained benefits.

There is a further qualification of the limits. Irrespective of the amounts of any benefits which an employee has retained, his current employer may provide him with a pension of 1/60th of final remuneration for each year of service with the employer, up to a maximum of 40 years. The employee may commute all or part of his pension for a lump sum which does not exceed 3/80ths of final remuneration for each of those years of service. This facility is of particular interest to someone who retires on pension from an occupation with an early NRD, such as one of the armed forces, and takes up a new employment at a salary which is less than one-and-a-half times the pension from the previous employment.

Early retirement

A member may retire early at any age, by reason of incapacity, and may receive immediate benefits in the same proportions of final remuneration as would have applied at his NRD.

A member may retire early, otherwise than by reason of incapacity, if he is at least 50 years old, and receive immediate benefits. And a woman whose NRD is earlier than age 60 may retire up to ten years before NRD, but not before she is 45 years old. The member may receive immediate benefits which do not exceed a pension of 1/60th of final remuneration for each year of service, up to a maximum of 40 years, and may commute all or part of the pension for a lump sum which does not exceed 3/80ths of final remuneration for each year of service, up to a maximum of 40 years.

The pension and lump sum may alternatively be calculated by reducing the corresponding figures for the member's NRD in the ratio of the number of actual years of service (with a maximum of 40) to the number of years of potential service to NRD (limited to 40, if so desired).

Late retirement

A member who remains in service after NRD may be provided with additional benefits to bring the aggregate, expressed as a pension, up to the maximum which would be approvable if the actual retirement date were the NRD. If the total service exceeds 40 years, each year in excess of 40 falling after NRD may earn an extra 1/60th of final remuneration up to a total maximum of 45/60ths of final remuneration at the actual retirement date.

Instead, a pension may be provided equal to the maximum which could have been payable at NRD, increased for the period of deferment either in line with the cost of living or actuarially by a factor relating to the yield of the scheme's investments or of the policy, as appropriate.

Lump sum benefits may be increased similarly to pension benefits. And if a member chooses to receive either pension or lump sum at NRD and to defer payment of the other, the part deferred may be increased. But if the member chooses to take any of the benefits at NRD, or subsequently before retirement, no further benefits can be available at retirement except insofar as those already taken fell short of the maximum then approvable, plus a cost of living increase (or alternatively an actuarial increase). If any benefit already taken included a lump sum, all subsequent benefits must be in the form of non-commutable pension: a second bite at the cherry is not allowed.

Death benefits

If a member dies in service, there may be provided a lump sum which does not exceed the greater of

(a) £5,000, and
(b) four times the member's final remuneration

plus a refund of any contributions the member has made to the scheme, with interest.

There may also be provided a widow(er)'s or dependant's pension which does not exceed two-thirds of the maximum pension the member could have received on retirement owing to incapacity on the date of death, with no entitlement to retained retirement benefits from earlier employment. If the widow(er) or dependant is entitled to a pension in respect of an earlier employment of the member, this must be deducted from the maximum amount to which the widow(er) or dependant could otherwise have been entitled.

Pensions may be provided for two or more beneficiaries, provided that none of them receives more than the maximum referred to in the previous paragraph and that the aggregate of all the pensions does not exceed one-and-a-half times that maximum.

If a member dies in retirement, the limits to a widow(er)'s or dependant's pension are similar to those quoted above, but are related to the maximum pension which the member could have received at retirement, in the particular circumstances in which retirement occurred (increased in line with the Retail Prices Index, for the period since retirement). No lump sum can be payable, except that an amount equal to the balance of five years' instalments of the member's pension may be payable on the member's death within that period.

Cost of living increases

Each of the pensions referred to in this summary may be increased, while in payment, in line with the Retail Prices Index or, alternatively, by 3 per cent per annum.

Glossary

This glossary includes some expressions which relate to pension schemes and personal pensions but which do not appear in this book. The remaining entries appear in one or more of the chapters.

Accrued rights Benefits under a pension scheme to which a member has become entitled because of his service up to a given date.

Actuary A specialist in the application of mathematics to life assurance and pensions who is a Fellow either of the Institute of Actuaries or of the Faculty of Actuaries.

Additional component The earnings-related element in the state pension.

Additional voluntary contribution (AVC) A contribution which a member makes to a scheme voluntarily in addition to the contribution (if any) which the scheme rules (or the rules of another scheme which relates to his employment) require him to make.

Administrator The person or persons resident in

the UK having the management of a personal or occupational pension scheme.

Annuity A contract by which an insurance company or friendly society undertakes to make a series of payments in a period which depends on the duration of one or more lives.

Appropriate scheme A scheme certified by the OPB as complying with the requirements of Schedule 1 to the Social Security Act 1986 for providers of personal pensions.

Approved scheme A personal or occupational pension scheme approved by the Board of Inland Revenue.

Augmentation The provision of occupational pension scheme benefits in excess of those which have been promised for a member.

Average salary scheme A scheme under which the benefits for a member are related to the average of his annual earnings during the years of his employment which entitle him to benefits.

Commutation Substitution of a single cash payment for an entitlement to payments of pension.

Contracted-out employment An employment for which a contracting-out certificate, issued by the OPB after being satisfied that there is an adequate occupational pension scheme, is still in force.

Contribution Payment made by an employer or by an employee to the cost of a personal or occupational pension scheme.

Cooling-off period A period of 14 days during which somebody who has applied for a personal pension may withdraw his application without financial loss.

Glossary

Deferred annuity An annuity which is due to commence at a future date in return for payment of a single premium or a series of periodical premiums.

Defined benefits scheme A scheme in which the members' benefits are based on a formula related to their pre-retirement earnings – usually a final salary scheme.

Defined contributions scheme A money purchase scheme in which the rate of contribution by employer and employee are defined.

Dependant A person who is financially dependent on another or was dependent before the other's death. A child is regarded as being dependent on a parent until attaining age 18 or subsequently completing full-time education.

Deposit administration A method of funding a pension by which contributions, less expenses, are accumulated with interest to provide benefits when they become due.

DHSS The Department of Health and Social Security, which is responsible for the payment of state pensions and for the rebating of part of NI contributions as minimum contributions to contracted-out personal pensions.

Earnings related element The part of the state pension which depends on the pensioner's previous earnings between upper and lower earnings limits.

Escalating pension A pension, the amount of which increases by a fixed percentage each year.

Exempt approved scheme An approved scheme which qualifies for additional tax concessions because it is established under irrevocable trusts.

Expectation of life The average duration of life of a

group of people of the same age and sex in accordance with a particular mortality table.

Final salary scheme (or **final pay scheme**) An occupational scheme which relates the benefits for each member in retirement to his earnings at or shortly before retirement.

Free-standing AVCs Additional voluntary contributions which are made to a scheme which is outside the employer's pension scheme and to which the employer does not contribute.

Friendly society A society registered under the Friendly Societies Acts and providing benefits for its members on such events as death or retirement. Friendly societies are subject to certain limitations on the amounts of benefits they may provide, and they qualify for certain tax advantages.

Funding The building up of a fund in advance which will provide benefits when they become due.

Gilt edged security An investment issued on behalf of the Government which provides a guaranteed rate of interest and usually provides for repayment of capital on a fixed date or within a defined period.

Golden handshake A cash payment which is made gratuitously by an employer – usually in connection with the termination of an employee's service. It is NOT part of a pension scheme.

Graduated pension Addition to the flat rate state pension which accrued between 6 April 1961 and 5 April 1975 for employees who were not in contracted-out employment.

Guaranteed minimum pension (GMP) The amount, approximately equal to the SERPS pension, which the rules of a contracted-out final salary scheme require that the scheme pension shall equal or exceed.

Glossary

Immediate annuity An annuity, payment of which begins at the appropriate interval after receipt of the purchase money by the insurance company or friendly society; eg a monthly annuity usually begins a month after receipt of the purchase money.

Incapacity Physical or mental deterioration which is bad enough to prevent an individual from following his normal employment, or which seriously impairs his earning capacity.

Insured scheme A scheme for which the contributions are paid as premiums for one or more insurance policies.

Irrevocable trust A trust which cannot be unilaterally dissolved, ie the creator of the trust cannot revoke or unscramble the trust.

Incentive payment See 'special incentive payment'.

Joint notice Form completed by earner and personal pension provider to notify the DHSS when it must commence making payments to the earner's personal pension scheme.

Lower earnings limit The level of earnings below which National Insurance contributions are not payable. It is approximately 25 per cent of national average earnings.

Member An individual for whom an occupational scheme provides benefits in respect of his current or previous employment.

Minimum contribution The DHSS contribution to a contracted-out personal pension.

Money purchase scheme A scheme in which each member's benefits are determined by the contributions made in respect of him and not by a benefit formula.

Mortality table A table prepared from statistical evidence and showing the probability of death occurring at each age in the table.

Net pay arrangement Arrangement by which an employer deducts an employee's contributions to an occupational pension scheme from his earnings before calculating PAYE tax thus giving tax relief on the contributions.

Net relevant earnings A person's earnings, net of prescribed deductions, on which the permitted maximum contributions to a personal pension or his maximum qualifying contributions for a self-employed pension are based.

NI contributions National Insurance contributions, payment of which is a prior condition for entitlement to state pensions.

NI rebate Payment made by the DHSS to a personal pension provider in respect of NI contributions made by the earner and employer.

Normal retirement date/age (NRD/NRA) The date/age at which a member is expected to retire, in accordance with the rules of an occupational scheme.

Occupational pension scheme A scheme which provides pensions by reason of its members' employment (other than self-employment) and to which their employers must normally contribute part, at least, of the cost.

Occupational Pensions Board (OPB) A body set up by the Social Security Act 1973 to advise the government on matters which concern occupational pension schemes and to carry out specified duties in relation to such schemes.

Open market option The option to transfer the value of pension benefits, when they become payable,

Glossary

to an insurance company chosen by the pensioner, usually because it will provide a larger pension.

Paid-up pension A pension which is not yet payable but for which no further contributions are to be made.

Pay-as-you-go A system by which pensions are paid out of current contributions instead of from accumulated funds, eg the state scheme in the UK.

Pension (in relation to a member of an occupational pension scheme) A series of payments made at regular intervals either to a former employee or to the widow(er) or a dependant by reason of the former employment.

Pension (in relation to a personal pension) A series of payments made at regular intervals, either to the earner or to the widow(er) or a dependant, after the earner's death, by reason of contributions made by the earner, and possibly by the employer and/or DHSS.

Pensionable age See 'State pensionable age'.

Pensionable employment Employment which qualifies an employee for an occupational pension.

Premium A single or periodical payment which a policy holder makes to an insurance company or friendly society to buy benefits which the policy will provide.

Preservation A continuing entitlement to deferred retirement benefits for a member whose employment has terminated.

Protected rights Rights purchased by NI rebates, special incentive payments and transfer payments insofar as they represent such rebates or incentive payments.

Purchased life annuity An annuity bought with money which the annuitant had complete freedom to use, including a lump sum obtained by commuting part of a pension. The annuity is taxable only on the part of each instalment which represents interest.

Pure endowment A policy which provides a given sum at the end of a given period. If death occurs within the period, the insurance company either pays nothing or refunds premiums received, depending on the terms of the policy.

Qualifying service Service which counts towards the establishment of a right to the preservation of retirement benefits on the termination of an employment.

Retained benefits Benefits which have been paid (or are payable) under another scheme (including a personal pension) and which must be taken into account in determining the approvable benefits under a particular occupational scheme.

Retirement annuity The term by which Chapter III Part XIV of the Income and Corporation Taxes Act 1988 refers to a self-employed pension policy.

Retirement benefits scheme The term by which Chapter I Part XIV of the Income and Corporation Taxes Act 1988 refers to what is commonly known as an occupational pension scheme.

Reversionary bonus A bonus added to a basic benefit under a policy and payable at the same time and in the same way as the benefit.

Salary related pension scheme An average or final salary (or pay) scheme.

Schedule D The part of the Income and Corporation Taxes Act 1988 which refers to the method of taxing various sources of income, including the earnings of people carrying on a business or profession on their own or in partnership.

Schedule E The part of that Act which refers to the method of taxing earnings of employees.

Secretary of State for Social Services The cabinet minister who is responsible for the DHSS.

Section 21 orders Orders made by the Secretary of State, in accordance with section 21 of the Social Security Pensions Act 1975, for revaluing earnings factors used for determining GMPs and SERP pensions.

Section 32 policy Policy issued by an insurance company in accordance with section 32 of the Finance Act 1981 to a former member of an occupational pension scheme, on receiving a transfer payment made by the trustees of the scheme to extinguish their liability in respect of the member.

SERPS The state earnings related pension scheme which was established by the Social Security Pensions Act 1975 and started on 6 April 1978.

Shopping option Another name for an open market option.

Short service benefit A retirement benefit preserved for a member whose employment terminates before normal retirement age.

Special incentive payment Payments made by the DHSS to personal pensions and occupational pensions providers in respect of employees who become contracted out between 1 January 1986 and 5 April 1993 and are not disqualified by reason of earlier contracted-out employment.

Speculative investments Investments which offer the prospect of above-average profit, accompanied by

The Pensions Revolution

an above-average risk of loss.

Sponsored superannuation scheme An occupational pension scheme to which the employer contributes.

State earnings related pension scheme SERPS

State pensionable age The commencement age for state pensions, ie 60 for women and 65 for men.

Superannuation Funds Office (SFO) The part of the Inland Revenue which grants approval, for tax purposes, of personal and occupational pension schemes and self-employed pension policies.

Term assurance A life assurance policy under which the sum assured is payable only if the life assured dies within a given period.

Terminal bonus A bonus added when a retirement benefit becomes payable.

Transfer value A cash sum paid by the party responsible for payment of personal or occupational pension benefits to transfer responsibility to another party.

Unit-linked policy A policy, the benefits under which depend on the numbers of units in the funds of the insurance company which are allocated when the policy holder pays premiums and the value of those units when benefits become payable.

Unit trust An investment trust which issues units for public sale, the units being a measure of a holder's interest in the trust's investments.

Upper band earnings Earnings between the lower and upper earnings limits.

Upper earnings limit The level of earnings in

excess of which no further National Insurance contributions are payable by an employee: it is between 6.5 and 7.5 times the lower earnings limit.

Index

(References to employers and employees are too frequent for them to be usefully included in the index.)

actuary, 20, 41, 66-8, 89
additional voluntary contribution (AVC), 32-4, 42, 47, 77, 89, 92
annuity, 28, 40, 67, 90-1, 93, 96
appropriate scheme, 40, 73, 90
average pay scheme, 19, 90, 97

bank, 14, 54, 58-9, 65-6, 79
bonuses, 55-7, 67, 96, 98
building society, 54, 58-9

capital gains, 18, 57
compound bonus, 55-6
contracting-out, 11, 17-18, 27-30, 32, 34-5, 37-40, 50-1, 71-9, 90-3, 98
contributions, 13, 18-22, 29, 31-5, 37, 39-44, 50-1, 54-6, 58-9, 61-3, 72-5, 78-80, 88, 90-1, 93-5

death benefit, 27-30, 39-40, 43-4, 51-2, 54-5, 66-7, 72, 78-9, 82-3, 87-8, 92, 95
deferred annuity, 57, 91
defined benefits scheme, 19-20, 54, 67-8, 71-2, 75, 81, 91
defined contribution scheme, 21, 81, 91

dependant, 27-9, 39-40, 51-2, 54-5, 77, 79, 88, 91, 95
deposit account, 58-9
deposit administration, 57-62, 67, 91
DHSS, 11, 18, 31-2, 34-5, 37, 40, 51, 54, 63, 72-3, 75-6, 80, 91, 93, 95, 97
directors, 21, 81

early retirement, 10, 28, 86
European Economic Community, 48

final salary scheme, 19-20, 22, 78-9, 91-3, 97
Finance Act, 1970, 38, 43
Finance (No 2) Act, 1987, 22-3, 33, 35, 38, 40, 43
Financial Services Act, 1986, 7, 14, 46
flat rate state pension, 15-6, 18, 26, 31, 43, 45, 48, 92
friendly society, 28-9, 40, 54, 57-9, 90, 92-3, 95

group personal pension scheme, 23, 51, 79
guaranteed minimum pension (GMP), 55, 71-2, 75, 93, 97

101

Index

hybrid scheme, 21-2, 78-9

ill health, 27, 43
incapacity, 28, 86, 88, 93
incentive payment 34-5, 74, 76, 93, 96-7
Income and Corporation Taxes Act, 1970, 22-3
Income and Corporation Taxes Act, 1988, 38, 96-7
inflation, 11, 13, 16-17, 21-2, 72, 83
information dissemination, 48-51, 80
inheritance tax, 28, 30, 44
Inland Revenue (IR), 27, 29, 32-3, 38-43, 81-8, 90, 98
insurance broker, 14, 79
insurance company, 14, 28-9, 40, 54-61, 63-8, 75, 90, 93, 95-8
interest rate, 18, 53, 58, 60, 92
interim bonus, 56
investment, 13, 19-21, 39, 51, 53-69, 71, 76, 87, 92
irrevocable trust, 39, 92-3

job changing, 10-11, 22, 75, 78-80

late retirement, 26, 87
leaving scheme, 30, 52, 75, 81
life assurance, 43-4, 55, 67, 89, 98
lower earnings limit, 15, 17, 38, 72, 74, 91, 93, 99
lump sum, 27, 29, 40, 43-4, 55, 57-8, 83-8, 96

managed fund, 65-6
maximum contribution, 33-5, 41-2
minimum contribution, 30, 34, 37-8, 40, 51, 91, 93
money purchase, 21-2, 50, 54, 72-3, 76, 78-9, 91, 94

National Insurance (NI) contribution, 16, 32, 34, 37-8, 72-3, 91, 93-4, 99
National Insurance Fund, 15-16
net pay arrangement, 42, 94
normal retirement age/date (NRA/NRD), 28, 82-4, 86-7, 94, 97

Occupational Pensions Board (OPB), 38-40, 71, 90, 94
occupational pension scheme, 8, 11-12, 14, 17-22, 26-8, 30, 32-5, 38-9, 41-3, 47-52, 54, 63-8, 71-3, 75, 77-81, 89-98
old age pension, 15

part-time work, 47-8
PAYE, 34, 42-3, 94
pension consultant, 14, 30, 67
pension provider, 14, 23, 29-30, 32, 40, 42, 51, 54, 58, 60-2, 68, 73-7, 93-4, 97
personal pension, 7, 11, 18, 22-3, 28-30, 32, 34-5, 37-8, 40-4, 46, 50-2, 54-63, 67-8, 73-7, 80, 82, 89-91, 93-8
preserved benefit, 11, 22, 95-7
protected rights, 51, 54-5, 72-3, 75-6, 96
pure endowment, 57, 61, 96

rebate, 63, 72, 74, 76, 91, 94, 96
redundancy, 10
Retail Prices Index (RPI), 83, 85, 88
reversionary bonus, 56, 61, 96

Secretary of State for Social Services, 38, 97
self-administered scheme, 63, 68
self-employed, 22-3, 55, 85, 94, 98
simple bonus, 55-6

Index

simplified procedures, 32, 81
Social Security Act, 1973, 11, 38, 94
Social Security Act, 1985, 11
Social Security Act, 1986, 9, 11-12, 15, 17, 22, 31, 33, 59, 90
Social Security Pensions Act, 1975, 11, 17, 39, 71, 97
state earnings related pension scheme (SERPS), 9, 11, 15-17, 25-30, 32, 37-8, 47, 50-1, 71-3, 75-7, 93, 97-8
state pension age, 26, 32, 72, 98
Superannuation Funds Office (SFO), 38-40, 98

switching, 30, 62, 69

tax advantages, 18, 37-44, 47, 58, 92
terminal bonus, 57, 98
transfer payment, 28, 54, 58, 60, 62, 75, 95-8
trustee, 39, 42, 44, 49, 64-8, 97

upper earnings limit, 15, 38, 72, 74, 91, 99
unit linking, 60-3, 98
unit trust, 43, 54, 59-63, 66, 98

widow(er), 9, 27-9, 40, 54-5, 72-3, 79, 88, 95
with-profit policy, 55-8, 60-2